BIGGER
BOLDER
BAKING

BIGGER BOLDER BAKING

A Fearless Approach to
Baking Anytime, Anywhere

GEMMA STAFFORD

PHOTOGRAPHY BY CARLA CHOY

HOUGHTON MIFFLIN HARCOURT
BOSTON   NEW YORK   2019

For information about permission to reproduce selections from this book, write to trade.permissions@hmhco.com or to Permissions, Houghton Mifflin Harcourt Publishing Company, 3 Park Avenue, 19th Floor, New York, New York 10016.

hmhbooks.com

Library of Congress Cataloging-in-Publication Data

Names: Stafford, Gemma, author. | Choy, Carla, photographer.
Title: Bigger bolder baking / Gemma Stafford ; photography by Carla Choy.
Description: Boston : Houghton Mifflin Harcourt, 2019. | Includes index.
Identifiers: LCCN 2019002549 (print) | LCCN 2019002715 (ebook) | ISBN 9781328546388 (ebook) | ISBN 9781328546326 (paper over board)
Subjects: LCSH: Cooking, American. | Baking. | LCGFT: Cookbooks.
Classification: LCC TX715 (ebook) | LCC TX715 .S77526 2019 (print) | DDC641.81/5—dc23
LC record available at https://lccn.loc.gov/2019002549

Book design by Rae Ann Spitzenberger

Food and prop styling by Kate Martindale

Printed in China

C&C 10 9 8 7 6 5 4 3 2 1

Mum and Dad,
Which one of your other kids wrote a book??!
Love, Gemma

CONTENTS

INTRODUCTION

A HERITAGE OF BAKING

I pressed down on the crumb topping, feeling the slickness of rich Irish butter between my fingers. I was seven years old and standing on my tiptoes to reach the kitchen table as my mum taught me how to make her apple crumble, a quintessential Irish dessert. I did everything just as Mum instructed, and I was bursting with pride when it came out of the oven. Like everything we made, it was a bit of this and a handful of that, and it was glorious.

Baking, in my family, has always been about making do, about turning out something absolutely delicious no matter what obstacles lie in the way. With five children to feed, my large Catholic family was always bumping into each other in the kitchen, trying to get my mum's attention. Everyone had a job—I did the tasks that little hands were good for, like slowly

adding spoonful after spoonful of sugar to egg whites as they whipped into a pavlova under my mum's watchful eyes. Or she'd set me down on the kitchen floor with cookies in a bag and a rolling pin, which I'd use to bash the cookies into crumbs for a lemon cheesecake she was making for Sunday lunch.

My mum was an amazing cook, and she set the bar high for other mums. She knew how to improvise and worked with whatever resources she had at her disposal, and that meant she could make almost anything, even with a practically bare pantry, and only a bowl, a whisk, and a few small (but willing!) hands to help.

I watched my mum create spectacular desserts from just a few simple ingredients and soon enough I was doing it, too. But while my mum would make a loaf of white bread, I would tinker with the recipe and make a loaf stuffed with bacon and cream cheese. Or I'd transform a regular meringue by adding butterscotch and bananas. It was never enough for me to simply make a recipe—I always wanted to make it better or different.

As I grew up, I continued to spend time in the kitchen and I began to think about attending cookery school. My mum warned me that becoming a professional pastry chef was a tough road, but she didn't realize that everything she had taught me had already set the stage for a career I was more than excited to begin.

HEADING TO CULINARY SCHOOL

At nineteen years old, I went off to study professional cookery at Cathal Brugha Street, Dublin, an institute that focused on catering and hospitality. From there, I was thrilled to get the opportunity to attend Ballymaloe Cookery School in Shanagarry, County Cork. There I trained under celebrity chef, acclaimed cookbook author, and TV personality Darina Allen, who had been named 2005's Cooking Teacher of the Year by the IACP.

My mum and I had watched Darina's show *Simply Delicious* on Monday nights for years, and there I was, learning from her in person. Under her direction, an important lesson was ingrained in me: Do not cook by halves. Your ingredients and how you manipulate them are the only things that matter in the kitchen. Everything else is a distraction.

A BAKING PROFESSIONAL

With the incredible instruction I received under Darina and my own bold style of baking, I took off to conquer the world as a young new pastry chef. My first stop was a priest's priory on the north side of Dublin, which housed dozens of elderly priests. The kitchen had nothing but some bowls, wooden spoons, and a small handheld electric mixer. But that was familiar territory to me, and the priests adored dessert, so I was in heaven making homemade doughnuts, tea cakes, and Chelsea buns all day for those sweet old men. They all had such an appreciation for what I did—except for Father Green.

On my first day at the priory, I was told

After that, I realized that I could bake anywhere—there was no kitchen from which I couldn't turn out something I was proud of.

by the head priest, "Don't try and make him happy, because you won't." Father Green complained about *everything*, and he drove everyone batty, including me. One day, out of the blue, I received a phone call from Father Green's niece. She was calling to thank me—after a recent visit, he had spent the entire time describing the latest thing I'd baked for him in intricate detail, and all in positive, glowing terms. It remains one of my greatest accomplishments to this day.

Throughout this experience, my mum was always there to offer wisdom and the encouragement I needed to take the next culinary step. That next step led me to pack my bags and head to Tuscany, where I worked as a private chef in a family's villa. In that gorgeous region of Italy, I would spend my mornings in the village, buying locally grown fruits and vegetables and farm-raised meats. I can still taste the homemade gnocchi and prosciutto I would buy from the delicatessen. Even the herbs in the family's herb garden were like nothing I had ever tasted.

Then I was faced with an unexpected dilemma: the family asked me to make them fresh pasta for dinner. I had never made pasta from scratch before, and the tiny, outdated kitchen didn't even have a working fridge, never mind a pasta machine. With no internet access to rely on, I realized I would have to improvise. I took a pasta recipe from a book I found in the kitchen and tinkered with it, adding my bold style to an otherwise basic recipe. I

rolled the dough as thin as I could using a bottle of wine as a rolling pin. I did know that pasta should be dried before cooking so I looked around that barren, ancient space and started hanging strands of pasta anywhere I could—on broom handles, wooden spoons, any long object I could find. In the end, the whole experience turned into a labor of love, and it was some of the most delicious pasta I have ever eaten, even to this day.

CALIFORNIA DREAMING

After that, I realized I could bake anywhere—there was no kitchen from which I couldn't turn out something I was proud of. So I took off for Australia and worked at the Thredbo ski resort for a season, making salads, sandwiches, and other hearty meals for hungry skiers. It was the first, and probably last, job where I rode a chairlift to work.

But I had my eye on living in the United States, and when I was offered a job as a bread baker at a South Lake Tahoe casino in California, I was thrilled. I was twenty-five years old and my shift started at three a.m., when most of my friends were only just getting home. But I didn't care—my goal was to learn the art of bread making, and in those wee hours of the morning, that's exactly what I did.

I fell in love with California, and when I was offered a pastry chef job at Spruce, a Michelin-starred restaurant in San Francisco, I dropped everything to take it. There, surrounded by chefs who were as ambitious and innovative as I was, I learned to love the hard rhythms of turning out Michelin-worthy desserts every day. Again, I was up at the crack of dawn to get all the dough going and spin ice creams in the cold, early-morning kitchen. It was as hard as my mum had warned, but the knowledge I gained and the friendships I made there made it all worth it—I think there's something about being paid minimum wage that really bonds people.

As time went by, I found myself working every hour I wasn't sleeping, but I could barely pay my rent. I decided to quit and start a catering business, which I hoped would allow me to stay in San Francisco without having to work 24/7. The experiences I had at each job had made me a wiser and more experienced chef. I knew food, and what I didn't know about business I was confident I could make up as I went along. My business was quickly hired by a Silicon Valley tech company to serve breakfast to their engineers, which I later found out meant, "Lure the engineers into actually getting to work at nine a.m. by cooking something mind-blowing." The added twist? The "kitchen" was two toaster ovens and a hot plate, and I had sixty busy engineers to feed. But by then, I had spent years cooking in kitchens all over the world—this wasn't my first rodeo. I knew I could wow those engineers. I turned that dorm room–style kitchen into a breakfast experimentation lab. When I started serving breakfast, only a few people would show up before nine, and the

rest would trickle in around ten. I noticed that Friday was the most challenging day because most people were already checked out for the weekend, and decided to rise to the challenge—by god, I was going to get them into the office! One Friday I made red velvet pancakes with cream cheese frosting (page 89). Needless to say, those engineers practically lost their minds with joy. Word got out around the office that Friday was the day to show up early, and after that, slowly but surely, they all started showing up. I continued to push myself, trying to outdo the Friday pancakes and get even more creative for Monday through Thursday's breakfasts as well. Soon every one of those hungry engineers was showing up to work early so they could eat what became known as a "Gemma breakfast."

As you can probably tell by now, I love a challenge, and soon I was ready for a new one. But I had done it all: I'd baked everywhere from a Michelin-starred kitchen to a hot-plate-in-an-office kitchen. Through it all, I'd been collecting recipes in dozens of old notebooks and wishing I could share the shortcuts I was inventing and the little tips and tricks I was teaching myself with a wider audience. After a decade of working as a professional chef, I felt I had a lot to share. But where to from here? It was 2014, and the internet was making the world a smaller place. I thought, *If I'm going to teach people how to bake, why not reach them online?*

And so, Bigger Bolder Baking was born.

TAKING IT ONLINE

I wanted my next move to be something new—something visual. I still wanted to bake but I didn't want to be standing in a kitchen at five o'clock in the morning. My husband, Kevin, who has worked in the entertainment industry his entire career, said, "Why don't we join forces and marry the two things we are both passionate about—food and entertainment?" And that's when we created our online show, *Bigger Bolder Baking*.

Let me just start by saying that we quit our full-time jobs and moved cities to start this new career, and we didn't have a clue what we were doing. All we knew was that whatever we *didn't* know, we'd have to learn, and fast.

Bigger Bolder Baking has a simple premise. Most food television shows have strayed from teaching people how to cook and are focused more on competition. I saw a need for a high-quality online show that actually taught people how to bake, whatever their skill level or equipment and pantry items in their kitchens. I use my cherished recipes, which have been perfected through years of making them in every kind of kitchen imaginable, to teach my audience the basics and beyond.

We started creating videos in our tiny kitchen in Santa Monica, California. Kevin had never produced a show before and I had never hosted . . . anything?? I didn't blink for the first few episodes because I was scared stiff. But I knew I had excellent baking skills, and I got through each episode by talking about the techniques I used and sharing the useful tips I had learned—along with great recipes, of course. Eventually, I got used to the camera and started blinking like a normal human being, and soon enough, it all became second nature to me. It helped that I was talking about a topic I loved, and isn't that half the battle?

Once a week, Kevin and I launched a new video on YouTube. We did everything on the show—soup to nuts—and we made do with what little we had, whether it was kitchen equipment or production equipment. Somehow, we managed to make it work. Slowly but surely, week after week, people began tuning in, and we started to build a following. It turned out our instincts were right: There were others out there who wanted to learn the traditional baking skills I had mastered. They loved my tips about things like reusing butter paper to grease your baking tin, or found my Fudgiest Giant Brownies (page 162) on a quest for the perfect brownie recipe. These were my people!

As my following grew, viewers began to get to know me as much as my food, and today they have become this wonderful tribe of deeply loyal fans who call themselves "Bold Bakers."

We became one of the fastest-growing baking shows online and have one of the best baking communities. My recipes have been seen and shared all over the world

These recipes are simplicity itself, and will show that you can end the day with something sweet no matter what stands in your way.

on all media platforms, and I have been featured on many media outlets including the Food Network, *The Doctors*, and even on Netflix's show *Nailed It!*

ANYONE CAN BECOME A BOLD BAKER

So here I am, sharing my treasure trove of recipes with you in *Bigger Bolder Baking*, my debut cookbook. These are the recipes I grew up on and those I invented and perfected while traveling the world. They're the recipes I make every day in my home in sunny California. And nearly every recipe calls for less than ten ingredients and no more than four everyday kitchen tools. They are simplicity itself, and will show that you can end the day with something sweet no matter what stands in your way. They represent my culinary journey and the bootstrapping attitude that has so defined my work as a chef, baking personality, and YouTube star.

At its core, "Bold Baking" is an ode to spontaneous baking with over-the-top flavors, all put together with very little fuss. That means to make these recipes, you won't need any special equipment, rare spices, anxiety-inducing techniques, or unpronounceable ingredients you'll use only once. *Bigger Bolder Baking* is about getting back to the essential, simplest components of baking—flour, sugar, butter, heat—and delighting you with more than one hundred utterly marvelous things you can make with them. It restores baking to an everyday art rather than relegating it to a weekend-only indulgence, and it reminds us that a few bites of a freshly made dessert can (and should) be a daily pleasure.

INGREDIENTS, TECHNIQUES, TOOLS & SUBSTITUTIONS

OVER THE YEARS, I'VE DONE A TREMENDOUS AMOUNT of baking, and I've gone back to some key ingredients, techniques, and tools again and again. If you're new to baking, think of this as a checklist for stocking your kitchen and a simple primer to teach you the basic skills you'll need to make the recipes in this book. More experienced bakers will find much here to add to their knowledge as well.

Ingredients

These are the ingredients I always have in my pantry or fridge, at the ready for spontaneous baking.

BUTTER

Recipes often call for softened butter, and avid bakers should always have some out at room temperature (68° to 70°F). I usually leave the amount I need at room temperature overnight to ensure it's soft enough to use the next day. If you haven't thought that far ahead (and believe me, sometimes I don't), leave the butter at room temperature for about 1 hour before using, or pop it into the microwave for just a few seconds. Cold butter won't mix with other ingredients as well as softened butter will, meaning your final baked good might not be as airy or rise as high as it should.

Salted vs. Unsalted A lot of bakers use unsalted butter so they can have more control over the total amount of salt used in a recipe. However, I have always used salted butter in my baking while still adding whatever amount of salt is called for in a recipe. Unless your recipe calls for a great deal of butter, salted or unsalted won't make or break the recipe. At the end of the day, it comes down to your personal preference.

BUTTERMILK

The acid in buttermilk tenderizes the gluten in flour and it's what makes many cakes and biscuits so delightfully soft and tender. I use it often in my cake recipes. Naturally acidic ingredients like sour cream and yogurt can be substituted for buttermilk (see page 308). You can also make an easy substitute by mixing regular dairy milk with lemon juice or vinegar (see page 308).

Sometimes it's hard to find smaller cartons of buttermilk, which can be inconvenient when a recipe calls for only a couple of tablespoons. I started freezing leftover buttermilk and now I always have it on hand whenever I need it for dressings, pancakes, and marinades. Freeze 1 to 2 cups in small containers, and don't forget to write the date and quantity on each. Every time you need it, it will be waiting. Thaw the frozen buttermilk in the refrigerator before using.

CHOCOLATE

There are dozens of varieties of chocolate at the store now, but how to know which one to buy? Bittersweet? Semisweet? 50% cacao? 80% cacao? When you understand what the cacao percentages mean, you'll have an easier time choosing the perfect chocolate for whatever you plan to bake. The percentage listed on the label is an indicator of the percentage of chocolate liquor and cacao solids (that is, the chocolate components) the chocolate contains in relation to other ingredients (such as sugar or milk). The higher the percentage, the darker and less sweet the chocolate. In each recipe, I specify which type of chocolate and cacao percentage is best to use.

Milk Chocolate (38 to 42%) This is the type most commonly found in commercial candy bars. It's one of the sweetest varieties because it has a higher sugar content and therefore tastes less chocolaty. Milk chocolate can have as little as 10% cacao, though most live within the 38 to 42% range. If you don't like chocolate with any bitterness, then this is for you.

Semisweet (52 to 62%) Semisweet chocolate is an entry-level choice for those who are new to darker chocolate with more pronounced flavor. Most chocolate chips, a standard ingredient in many kitchens, fall within this range. With a sweet flavor and creamy consistency, semisweet is a dream to work with. It melts easily, combines well with other flavors, and is fantastic for dipping when melted.

Bittersweet (63 to 72%) This is my go-to chocolate, and I love the depth of flavor you get in any of my recipes that use it. It melts beautifully and is the key ingredient in my chocolate cookies. A square of bittersweet chocolate left to melt in my mouth is my idea of heaven.

Unsweetened (100%) As the name implies, unsweetened chocolate has 100% cacao solids with no added sugar or other ingredients. Often called baking chocolate, one taste will tell you that it's not meant to be eaten on its own. I like to use a small amount of it in combination with semisweet or bittersweet to add depth of flavor. If you make the mistake of buying unsweetened chocolate without realizing it, it's okay to throw a little into your baking; you may need to add a little extra sugar to your recipe to account for the added bitterness. Sometimes I use a mix of bittersweet and unsweetened chocolates in a ratio of 2 parts bittersweet to 1 part unsweetened to achieve the perfect balance of sweetness.

White Chocolate This type contains cocoa butter but not any of the cocoa solids of other chocolate, so it's not technically considered chocolate. It is much lighter in color than milk or dark chocolate because it contains no cocoa powder. It tastes nothing like other chocolate for the same reason, so don't try to use it as a substitute. Its sweetness works really well in my White Chocolate & Mascarpone Mousse (page 232).

Note Some of my recipes call for chocolate shavings for an easy decoration. To make these, simply use a vegetable peeler to shave off bits from a bar of chocolate.

COCOA POWDER

Cocoa powder is the chocolate remaining after cocoa butter is extracted from cacao beans. It's a pantry staple for any Bold Baker!

Natural unsweetened This is pure chocolate. It's the most common type, with an intense flavor, and I like to bake with it on a day-to-day basis. Just be sure to buy unsweetened cocoa.

Dutch-process Cocoa powders labeled "Dutch-process" or "European-style" have been treated to neutralize the cocoa's naturally occurring acids, giving it a mellower flavor and a redder color. Since Dutch-process cocoa isn't acidic, it doesn't react with alkaline leaveners like baking soda to produce carbon dioxide. That's why recipes that use Dutch-process cocoa are usually leavened with baking powder instead of baking soda.

COFFEE

To achieve an intense coffee flavor in my recipes, I use dried instant coffee granules diluted in a tiny amount of water. I still get a powerful punch of coffee flavor without having to add too much extra liquid. For recipes like My Family's Favorite Tiramisu (page 257), I mix instant coffee granules with enough water to create a mug of "brewed coffee" that's just right for dipping the ladyfingers.

CORNSTARCH

Extracted from corn, cornstarch is fantastic for thickening sauces, puddings, and pie fillings. It's flavorless and colorless. To use it, mix it with a little water or another liquid before adding it to your recipe, which will keep it from developing lumps. After adding cornstarch to a recipe, the mixture needs to be brought to a boil to thicken properly. In the UK, cornstarch is known as "corn flour"; in the US, "corn flour" refers to finely milled cornmeal, a different product entirely.

CREAM

There are many different types of cream, and they're often called different names in different countries, making it even more confusing. Wherever you live, look for the fat content on the package to make sure you're buying the one you need.

20% fat Sometimes labeled as "light cream" or "single cream," it has a relatively low fat content that is not high enough for whipping. It can be used for my Silky-Smooth Chocolate Soup (page 100) or Signature Salted Caramel Sauce (page 288), or for pouring into your morning cup of coffee. I've also seen it sold as "table cream."

30% fat Commonly known as "whipping cream," the fat content in this cream is high enough to allow it to thicken, but ironically, it's not the best for whipping into stiff peaks. I use this cream in my Salted Butterscotch Pots de Crème (page 107) and Vanilla Panna Cotta with Roasted Strawberries (page 110). This cream is not ideal for my Three-Ingredient No-Churn Vanilla Ice Cream (page 236) because it doesn't whip up firm enough.

36% fat Often called "heavy cream" or "heavy whipping cream," this is my choice for most of my recipes. It has the highest fat content so it whips up very well—it will double in volume—and holds its shape. It's best used for desserts that need a really sturdy whipped cream, like my Lemon Curd Mousse (page 235) and my Three-Ingredient No-Churn Vanilla Ice Cream (page 236).

EGGS

Room-temperature eggs incorporate better with other ingredients like flour and sugar, which are already at room temperature, and egg whites will whip up much fluffier if you're making meringue. To take the chill off your eggs in a hurry, place them in a bowl of warm water and let them sit for about 5 minutes before using.

Egg whites I call for a lot of egg whites in my recipes. If I happen to have any left over from making a custard, for example (which uses only yolks), I put them in a zip-top plastic bag, press out the air, label them with the amount and the date, and freeze them for up to 5 months. To thaw, I put them in the fridge overnight or let them sit at room temperature for 4 hours. They whip up beautifully every time!

If you have a bowl of egg whites but don't know how many are in there, don't worry! A whole egg weighs about 60 grams: about one-third yolk and two-thirds white, meaning 20 grams for the yolk and 40 grams for the white. Weigh the egg whites and then divide by 40 to get the number of whites.

FLOUR

There are dozens of different flours available; each one has a different purpose and will yield different results in your baked goods. It's important to use the specific flour called for in each recipe (or use an appropriate substitute). I use the following varieties the most in my recipes.

All-purpose flour (plain flour, white flour) Exactly like it sounds, this is your everyday, go-to baking flour, and you'll use it for most recipes. The protein content of this flour is between 9 and 11 percent, which is more than cake flour and less than bread flour, so it's an appropriate choice for everything from cookies and bars to muffins and pie crust (hence the name "all-purpose"). I like to use unbleached all-purpose flour, which has not been chemically treated to whiten and "soften" the flour.

Bread flour (strong flour) Bread flour has a higher protein content than all-purpose flour (usually 11 to 13 percent), and as you would expect, it's used for making bread because the higher the protein content, the more gluten the flour produces. Gluten is what gives bread its structure and, together with yeast, creates the chewiness and airy texture everyone looks for in a loaf. If you don't have bread flour, you can use all-purpose flour, but keep in mind that you might not need the same amount of liquid in your recipe (see Substitutions, page 36).

Cake flour This is a finely milled, very low-protein (usually 8 to 10 percent) flour used primarily for cakes because it produces less gluten and results in a tender, fluffy crumb. It's most commonly seen in American recipes. It is very easy to make at home by mixing cornstarch with all-purpose flour (see page 303).

Self-rising flour This flour is really just all-purpose flour with baking powder added, and is used for quick breads, biscuits, and other baked goods that need an additional chemical leavener to rise properly. It should only be used when a recipe specifically calls for it. Don't use it interchangeably with all-purpose flour, because it will throw off the quantity of baking powder in your recipe. You can make it at home by mixing baking powder and all-purpose flour (see page 304). So easy!

Whole wheat flour Whole wheat flour is less processed than all-purpose, retaining the bran and germ, which is why it's often considered a healthier flour. It's also higher in fiber and oil content, which can make it harder to work with on its own. Using whole wheat flour makes baked goods denser and heavier, so I recommend using a combination of equal parts whole wheat and all-purpose flours. Whole wheat flour tends to absorb more liquid than other flours, so be prepared to add more liquid to achieve the consistency called for in the recipe. Whole wheat flour should be kept in the fridge or freezer because its higher oil content can make it go rancid faster.

LEAVENING AGENTS

Leavening agents like baking powder and baking soda create a chemical reaction that gives baked goods lift and airiness. To get the results you want, it's important to follow the recipe exactly and use the specific leavening agent it calls for.

Substituting one for another will not yield the same results. That's why it's really important to keep the following ingredients stocked in your pantry:

Baking powder Baking powder's leavening properties are activated when it comes in contact with moisture, making your baked goods expand and rise. You can see the reaction if you mix it with a little water; it will bubble up and get fizzy.

Baking soda For baking soda to do its job, it needs to be activated by an acid like buttermilk, sour cream, or vinegar. To see the reaction, add a little baking soda to some vinegar and watch it bubble up and fizz.

Cream of tartar This is an acid used to stabilize egg whites when you whip up a meringue, or whipped heavy cream. In my recipes, I use cream of tartar as often as I do baking powder or baking soda, so make sure to have a little jar in your pantry at all times. However, an acid like lemon juice can be used as a substitute in a pinch (see Substitutions, page 37). If you don't have any cream of tartar, you can still make recipes that call for it, but your whipped cream just won't whip up as stiff and creamy, and your meringue might have a tendency to "weep," meaning a little liquid will begin to separate if you don't serve it right away.

Yeast Most often used in breads and doughs for some other baked goods, yeast is activated by liquid and/or heat. Several

types are available, including "active dry" and "instant," both of which come in granulated form. These types can be used interchangeably, though if you use instant yeast, you won't need to let the dough rise a second time. The most common way to activate active dry yeast is to add a liquid to it, like water or milk, that has been heated to about body temperature. If you are using instant yeast, like I do in my recipes, you can add it directly to the dry ingredients and it will activate when you mix in the wet ingredients. Fresh yeast comes in cake form and is found in the refrigerated section of the grocery store. The recipes in this book were made with instant yeast; if you're using fresh yeast, use twice the amount called for in the recipe to achieve the same level of rise.

MILK

To add tenderness, flavor, and moisture to baked goods, I love to use milk. I prefer whole (full-fat) milk for the best texture and taste, but in most cases, you can substitute 1% or 2% milk or dairy-free milk (see Substitutions, page 36).

MOLASSES

This is a sweet, thick, dark brown syrup with a distinctive hickory, tangy flavor that is used in a lot of holiday recipes like gingerbread cookies. Known as "treacle" in the UK, molasses will give your baked goods a deeper layer of sweet flavor, almost like dark caramel. At the store you'll see sweeter "light" molasses and less sweet "dark" molasses, which has had more sugar removed. A third type, blackstrap molasses, has had the most sugar removed and has a quite bitter taste. It's used mostly for medicinal purposes, and I don't recommend it for baking. Sulfur dioxide is sometimes added to molasses as a preservative, but it also makes the flavor less sweet. I prefer unsulfured molasses in my recipes, so watch for that on the label.

OIL

When it comes to sweet baking, a flavorless oil like vegetable, canola, or sunflower oil is your best bet. Oils with stronger flavors tend to overpower the other flavors in baked goods, which I try to avoid. Coconut oil can be used in some recipes, but it does have a distinct coconut flavor, so be aware of this if you plan to use it. I don't recommend using olive oil, which has too strong a flavor for the recipes in this book.

SALT

Just as important in sweet baking as it in savory cooking, salt highlights and enhances the flavors of the other ingredients with which it is mixed. Even a pinch will make all the difference to your cakes, cookies, and especially breads. I use regular table salt for my baking because its fine grain dissolves and blends well other ingredients.

SUGAR

I use three common sugars in my recipes: granulated sugar, confectioners' sugar, and brown sugar. There are other sugars at the store like turbinado and raw sugar, and you can use them in place of granulated sugar in the recipes, but they are less processed and coarser, which can alter the flavor and texture of your baked good. Those sugars are quite coarse, so they are not good for frosting or icing.

Granulated sugar (caster sugar) When I call for "sugar" in my recipes, this is the sugar I'm talking about, and it's the type I call for the most. It's fine enough to dissolve quickly when mixed into a batter and has a nice flavor.

Confectioners' sugar (powdered sugar, icing sugar) This is granulated sugar that has been finely ground into a powder. It is most commonly used for cookies and frostings because it dissolves almost instantly, leaving the mixture very smooth.

Brown sugar Moister than granulated sugar thanks to the addition of molasses, brown sugar adds caramel flavor to your baking. At the store you'll see light brown and dark brown sugars. They can be used interchangeably, but dark brown sugar has a little more molasses and will result in a deeper, stronger flavor in your baked good. If you forget to buy it, make it at home (see page 307) or substitute an equal amount of granulated sugar.

Note When measuring, I don't firmly pack brown sugar. Just like when measuring all ingredients, I fill the cup and level it off.

VANILLA EXTRACT

This is an essential ingredient for bakers, and one of my favorites. I think of it more as a seasoning than a flavoring because, like salt, it enhances and brings out the flavors of the other ingredients in whatever you're baking.

You will notice I am not shy when it comes to the quantity of vanilla I call for in my recipes. Vanilla enhances the chocolate flavor in The Fudgiest Giant Brownies (page 162) and when used in Three-Ingredient No-Churn Vanilla Ice Cream (page 236), the alcohol in the vanilla helps lower the freezing point of the ice cream just enough to keep it from freezing rock solid. When buying vanilla, look for "pure extract" and don't buy anything labeled as "essence." You want vanilla made from actual vanilla beans, not low-grade artificial flavorings, which are far inferior.

Many home bakers don't realize that you can make your own vanilla extract by soaking whole vanilla beans in a neutral alcohol (like vodka) for several months to develop flavor (see page 300). I encourage you to try it—I think it tastes better than what you can buy at the store, and you'll save money, too.

Techniques

These are the most common techniques in baking, and once you learn them, you'll be able to make all the recipes in this book.

BAIN-MARIE

I mention cooking over a "bain-marie" a lot in this book, but what is it? This classic French technique uses gentle heat to cook more delicate foods like chocolate or custard. Basically, you suspend a bowl with the ingredient over simmering water and allow it to melt or cook slowly, which keeps it from burning or scorching. You can buy pans called double boilers specifically made for this purpose, but you can easily set up a bain-marie with a saucepan and a heatproof bowl.

To create a bain-marie Bring some water to a simmer in a saucepan. Set a heatproof bowl, bigger than the mouth of the saucepan, over the simmering water, making sure the water doesn't touch the bottom of the bowl. Put the ingredients in the bowl as directed by the recipe and allow the heat of the steam below to melt or heat the ingredients in the bowl slowly and evenly.

BLIND BAKING

When making a pie or tart, sometimes it's important to prebake the crust before adding the filling. This is called blind baking. I do this with recipes like my Rhubarb & Orange Custard Tarts (page 134). Simply dock (prick) the pastry with a fork, line with parchment, and fill it with a weight like dried beans or rice before baking as directed in the recipe; the weights help prevent the dough from bubbling up or sliding down the side of the pie pan. Then remove the weights and continue to bake for 5 more minutes to fully brown the pastry. Or you can freeze the dough before baking it (as described below) instead of using weights to help it keep its shape.

Docking the pie dough Roll out your pie dough and press it into the pie pan. Shape the edge and prick the uncooked dough all over with the tines of a fork. This allows steam to be released during baking, which will prevent the pastry from rising up. Then line the crust with parchment and fill it with a weight like dried beans or rice before blind baking.

Blind baking frozen pie dough Roll out your pie dough and press it into the pie pan. Shape the edge, dock the dough with the tines of a fork, and then put the entire pie pan into the freezer for at least 2 hours instead of lining it with parchment and weights. Pop the pan into the oven straight from the freezer.

CREAMING

Beating butter and sugar together with a wooden spoon or an electric mixer is called creaming. As the ingredients combine, air is also incorporated into the mixture, and it will become very light and fluffy. Creaming is responsible for creating great textures in cookies, particularly crisp ones, and in cakes. Creaming by hand requires a strong arm, but a little elbow grease will make light work.

FOLDING

When you need to combine a very light, air-filled mixture like whipped cream or whipped egg whites into other ingredients, folding them in will incorporate them without losing the airiness you worked so hard to attain.

To fold Add the air-filled mixture to the bowl containing the ingredients you want to combine. Using a large thin-edged metal spoon, cut through the ingredients in the center of the bowl, lift up the mixture, and turn it over. Turn the bowl 90 degrees and repeat. Continue doing this until the mixture is fully combined.

KNEADING

Bread dough and pasta dough need to be pressed and stretched to develop the gluten and add strength to the dough. Kneading can be done by hand or using the dough hook on a stand mixer.

To knead by hand Place the dough on a floured surface. Using the heel of your hand, push the dough away from you, then fold the dough over itself and push it away with the heel of your hand again. Repeat, sprinkling the dough with a little flour if it gets sticky and occasionally rotating the dough 90 degrees, until the dough feels elastic and smooth.

To knead with a stand mixer Fit the mixer with the dough hook, put the dough in the bowl, and mix on medium speed until the dough is elastic and smooth. You may need to add a bit of flour if it's too sticky. If the dough crawls up the dough hook, stop the mixer and push the dough down with a spatula, then continue mixing.

PROOFING DOUGH

Used mostly in bread making, the term *proofing* refers to the second, or final, rising of the dough that happens after the dough has been shaped. During proofing, the fermentation of the yeast produces carbon dioxide gas, which makes the bread rise and creates its crumb.

To proof dough Place the shaped dough (whether in a pan or shaped free-form on a baking sheet) in a warm place (a little warmer than room temperature) without drafts in your kitchen and cover it with a clean kitchen towel to prevent a crust from forming. The dough should double in size; at that point, it's ready to be baked.

RUBBING BUTTER INTO FLOUR

I use this method when making dough for pie or tart crusts or the topping for a fruit cobbler—it's the first technique my mum ever taught me. You can also rub butter, sugar, and flour together to make a topping for a fruit crisp. The idea is to mix them together, but not too much. You want the butter mixture to look like coarse bread crumbs, with the butter fully distributed throughout the flour. When the crust is baked, the butter will melt and leave airy pockets, which is how crusts gets their flaky, tender texture.

To rub in butter by hand Literally rub the butter into the flour with clean fingers until the mixture looks like coarse bread crumbs.

To rub in butter with a pastry blender or fork Crush the butter against the bottom and sides of the bowl using a pastry blender or a fork.

To rub in butter with a food processor Pulse the ingredients together in short bursts, watching carefully so you don't overmix.

SIFTING

Sifting dry ingredients incorporates air into them and removes any lumps. For most of my recipes, sifting is not required to ensure success, but there are two ingredients I recommend you sift every time: cocoa powder and confectioners' sugar. These two ingredients tend to clump, so sifting them before adding them to the mixing bowl ensures your batter will be smooth.

TEMPERING

Tempering means taking two ingredients with different temperatures and make them more similar in temperature so they will combine more easily. For example, a recipe might call for adding raw eggs to a hot mixture. If you were to simply add the eggs and mix them in, the heat of the mixture could cook them before they are fully incorporated, leaving you with scrambled egg throughout the mixture. Tempering prevents this. The word *tempering* is also used to refer to a technique where chocolate is heated to a certain temperature, then cooled to another temperature, which results in a smooth, glossy finish. None of the recipes in this book require chocolate tempering.

To temper eggs While whisking, add a few spoonfuls of the hot mixture to the egg mixture and whisk quickly to combine thoroughly. This raises the temperature of the eggs without cooking them. At this point you can add the entire egg mixture to the hot mixture and combine them safely.

WHIPPING CREAM OR EGG WHITES

To make meringue or whipped cream, air is whipped into eggs or heavy cream using a whisk or an electric mixer. There are two consistencies I look for: soft peaks or stiff peaks.

Soft peaks This is most commonly referred to when whipping egg whites. Soft peaks form after a short period of whipping either by hand or with an electric mixer, resulting in fluffy whites that just barely hold their shape. The peak will flop over immediately when the whisk or the beaters are lifted.

Stiff peaks When you continue whipping the cream or egg whites, the peaks will get much stiffer until they hold their shape when the whisk or the beaters are lifted. Whipped cream is almost always whipped to stiff peaks.

Essential Tools

Honestly, you don't need that much equipment to bake the recipes in this book. This list includes everything I use, and you probably own most of these things already.

- [ ] *Rimmed baking sheet, 10 x 15-inch with 1-inch sides (for roulades and jelly rolls)*
- [ ] *Cookie sheets (2), 13 x 18-inch*
- [ ] *Square cake pan, 8-inch (for blondies)*
- [ ] *Rectangular cake pan, 9 x 13-inch (for brownies)*
- [ ] *Round cake pans (3), 6-inch (for triple-layer cakes)*
- [ ] *Round cake pans (2), 9-inch (for double-layer cakes)*
- [ ] *Loaf pan, 9 x 5 x 3-inch*
- [ ] *Cupcake/muffin pan, 12-well*
- [ ] *Pie pan, 9-inch*
- [ ] *Tart pans with removable bottoms (6), 4-inch*
- [ ] *Springform pan, 9-inch*
- [ ] *Nonstick skillet, 12-inch*
- [ ] *Saucepan, 2-quart/2-liter*

- [ ] *Mixing bowls, small, medium, and large*
- [ ] *Stand mixer or handheld electric mixer*
- [ ] *Kitchen scale*
- [ ] *Wire rack*
- [ ] *Measuring cups*
- [ ] *Measuring spoons*
- [ ] *Palette knife or offset spatula*
- [ ] *Pastry brush*
- [ ] *Large whisk*
- [ ] *Rolling pin*
- [ ] *Rubber spatulas*
- [ ] *Ruler*
- [ ] *Scissors*
- [ ] *Large fine-mesh sieve*
- [ ] *Wooden spoons*

Substitutions

The rule of thumb when making substitutions in baking is to replace an ingredient with the same volume called for in the recipe. One thing to remember is that some substitutions can change the flavor or texture of your final baked good, so you may need to adjust your expectations. This chart lists the most common ingredients I have successfully substituted at one time or another.

RECIPE CALLS FOR	SUBSTITUTE	HOW TO DO IT
All-purpose flour	Whole wheat flour	Substitute whole wheat flour for half the all-purpose flour called for in the recipe. If you increase that ratio, your baked goods will be very heavy.
All-purpose flour	Gluten-free all-purpose flour	Substitute in equal amounts. Nut flours have a different texture than all-purpose flour and they also absorb liquid differently, so they can't be substituted easily.
All-purpose flour	Bread flour	Substitute in equal amounts. However, bread flour absorbs liquid differently, so easy does it when adding liquid. Don't add all the liquid called for in the recipe at once—add it a little at a time until you reach the consistency described in the recipe.
Butter	Dairy-free butter Margarine	Substitute in equal amounts.
Eggs	Mashed banana Sweetened condensed milk Ground flaxseed	One large egg = roughly ¼ cup (4 tablespoons/60g/ 2 ounces), so you need to replace that volume in your recipe. **For cakes:** Replace each egg with ½ small banana, mashed. **For cookies:** Replace each egg with ¼ cup sweetened condensed milk. **For brownies:** Replace each egg with 1 tablespoon ground flaxseed mixed with 3 tablespoons water
Milk	Dairy-free milk, including nut milks and canned coconut milk	Substitute in equal amounts. Just be aware that some milks might change the flavor of the recipe slightly.
Honey	Maple syrup Agave syrup	Substitute in equal amounts. I use honey in many of the recipes in this book, so it's best to always have it on hand.

RECIPE CALLS FOR	SUBSTITUTE	HOW TO DO IT
Oil	Melted butter Melted margarine Melted dairy-free butter	Substitute in equal amounts.
Cream of tartar	Lemon juice Vinegar	Substitute 2 teaspoons lemon juice or vinegar for every 1 teaspoon cream of tartar called for in the recipe.
Gelatin, powdered	Agar-agar (powdered, flakes, or bars)	Powdered agar-agar can be substituted in equal amounts. If using flakes or bars, substitute 1 tablespoon agar-agar for every 1 teaspoon powdered gelatin called for in the recipe. In either case, agar can be temperamental, so you may need to experiment a bit to get the same results as you would with gelatin.
Fresh fruit	Frozen fruit	Substitute in equal amounts. Thaw the fruit and drain off any excess liquid before using. Look for frozen fruit with no sugar added.
Buttermilk	Sour cream Whole milk	Mix equal parts sour cream and whole milk to reach the volume of buttermilk called for in the recipe. (You can also make your own buttermilk by mixing milk with lemon juice or vinegar; see page 308.)
Mascarpone cheese	Cream cheese	Substitute in equal amounts. Cream cheese is not as rich as mascarpone, but it is a good substitute.
Brown sugar	Granulated sugar	Substitute in equal amounts. The finished baked good might not have as deep a flavor, but it will still taste very good. You can make your own brown sugar by mixing granulated sugar with molasses (see page 307).
Yeast	Not recommended	Some people advocate substituting baking soda or baking powder for yeast in some bread recipes, but it will not yield the same result. If you don't have yeast, I suggest choosing another recipe to bake.
Graham crackers	Digestive biscuits Plain vanilla cookies	Substitute in equal amounts. Graham crackers aren't so common in Europe.
Golden syrup	Maple syrup Honey	Substitute in equal amounts. Golden syrup is commonly used in Ireland, but it's not as common in the US. However, you can easily buy it online.
Cornstarch	Arrowroot powder	Substitute 2 teaspoons arrowroot powder for every 1 teaspoon cornstarch. Dissolve the arrowroot in water as you would the cornstarch before adding it to the recipe.

Chapter 1

WOODEN SPOON & BOWL

WHEN I WAS JUST A GIRL GROWING UP IN IRELAND, my mum would always say, "If you can read, you can cook." With that philosophy as her guiding light, she brought me, my sisters, and my brother into the kitchen when we were quite young, and one of the first things we learned how to bake was cookies. There's no need for fancy equipment, and all you really need are a spoon and a bowl. In fact, Mum also used to say that in France, chefs didn't use electric mixers—they always mixed by hand. The recipes in this chapter include a wide variety of cookies, from beloved treats from my childhood like Old-School Crunchy Biscuits (page 43) and Butter Whirl Biscuits (page 48), plus new favorites I picked up from my travels like Chewy, Gooey Oatmeal Raisin Cookies (page 41) and Triple Chocolate Chip Cookies (page 70)—plus a crumble and a cobbler because they're so easy to mix up in a bowl.

CHEWY, GOOEY OATMEAL RAISIN COOKIES

MAKES 28 COOKIES

½ cup (1 stick/ 115 grams) butter, softened

⅓ cup (71 grams) granulated sugar

½ cup (85 grams) dark brown sugar

1 large egg

1 teaspoon pure vanilla extract (optional)

1½ tablespoons honey

1 cup (142 grams) all-purpose flour

½ teaspoon salt

½ teaspoon baking powder

½ teaspoon baking soda

1 cup (142 grams) raisins

1 cup (85 grams) rolled oats

Soft in the center, crunchy on the outside—an oatmeal cookie doesn't get much better than this. I like to load them up with plump raisins, which helps keep their moist-and-chewy goodness. This recipe also works well using other dried fruits, so go ahead and experiment, if you're in the mood to try something a little different.

1   Preheat the oven to 350°F (180°C) and line two cookie sheets with parchment paper.

2   In a large bowl, cream together the butter and sugars with a wooden spoon until soft and light in color.

3   Add the egg, vanilla, and honey and mix until combined.

4   Stir in the flour, salt, baking powder, and baking soda.

5   Fold in the raisins and oats.

6   Using a tablespoon measure, scoop out heaping tablespoons of the dough, roll them into balls, and place them on the prepared cookie sheets (you should end up with roughly 28 cookies). Leave some space between the cookies, as they'll spread during baking.

7   Bake for 8 to 10 minutes, until lightly golden brown. When you see that gorgeous crackle on top, they are done. Err on the side of undercooked, and they will be perfect. Transfer to a wire rack to cool.

8   Store the cookies in an airtight container at room temperature for up to 3 days.

OLD-SCHOOL CRUNCHY BISCUITS

MAKES 36 COOKIES

1 cup (2 sticks/
225 grams) butter,
softened

¾ cup (170 grams) sugar

2 tablespoons golden
syrup

1 cup (142 grams)
self-rising flour
(see page 304)

2⅔ cups (225 grams)
rolled oats

1 teaspoon baking soda

¼ teaspoon salt

These cookies are perfectly balanced—crunchiness on the one hand and a sweet buttery-oaty flavor on the other. My mum used to make them all the time using a recipe she found in one of her old cookbooks. Sometimes she would spread melted chocolate over each cookie, though we also loved them without. They don't take very long to make, which is probably why we always brought them to sell at school bake sales. My mum shared the recipe with me and now it's my pleasure to pass it on to you.

1 Preheat the oven to 350°F (180°C) and line two cookie sheets with parchment paper.

2 In a large bowl, cream together the butter and sugar with a wooden spoon until soft and light in color.

3 Add the golden syrup and mix until combined.

4 Add the flour, oats, baking soda, and salt and mix until the dough comes together.

5 Using a tablespoon measure, scoop out heaping tablespoons of the dough, roll them into balls, and place them on the prepared cookie sheets. Leave some space between the cookies, as they'll spread during baking. Press down on each ball to form cookies about 1½ inches in diameter.

6 Bake for 12 to 14 minutes, until lightly golden brown.

7 Let the cookies cool on the cookie sheets for 10 minutes, then transfer to a wire rack.

8 Store the cooled cookies in an airtight container at room temperature for up to 4 days.

10-MINUTE VANILLA
REFRIGERATOR COOKIES

MAKES 16 COOKIES

½ cup (1 stick/115 grams) butter, softened

¾ cup (170 grams) sugar

1 large egg

1 teaspoon pure vanilla extract

1½ cups (213 grams) all-purpose flour

1 teaspoon baking powder

When I was a young baker and just learning, I practiced my newfound skills with this simple recipe. Refrigerator cookies—what could be easier than that? What makes these cookies so great is that you can keep the dough at the ready in the fridge or freezer, slice it, and bake the cookies for only 10 minutes, making them as good as their name. Give them a go, and you'll see what I mean. The dough keeps in the fridge for up to a week or in the freezer for up to 2 months.

1 In a large bowl, cream together the butter and sugar with a wooden spoon until soft and light in color.

2 Beat in the egg and vanilla.

3 Add the flour and baking powder and mix to combine.

4 Shape the dough into a log roughly 8 inches long and wrap in plastic wrap or parchment paper. Roll it back and forth to create a sausage shape 2 inches in diameter. Refrigerate for at least 1 hour or up to 1 week.

5 Preheat the oven to 350°F (180°C) and line two cookie sheets with parchment paper.

6 Slice the chilled dough into ½-inch-thick rounds and place them on the prepared cookie sheets. Leave some space between the cookies, as they'll spread during baking.

7 Bake for 10 to 12 minutes, until golden brown. Transfer to a wire rack to cool.

8 Store the cookies in an airtight container at room temperature for up to 3 days.

BIGGER BOLDER IRISH SHORTBREAD

MAKES 16 COOKIES

1 cup plus 2 tablespoons (2¼ sticks/255 grams) butter, softened

½ cup (115 grams) sugar

2 cups (283 grams) all-purpose flour

1 cup (115 grams) cornstarch

I have three sisters and one brother, and when we were kids, we all loved to mess about in the kitchen. In fact, each of us had a specialty: Suzanne made the best chocolate cakes; Julie baked carrot cake; George was always making profiteroles; and I love to make all different kinds of cookies. Carol-Ann didn't bake all that much, but she was the one who always made shortbread. I can still remember her patting the dough into the "shortbread pan," a very old 8-inch round baking tin that had been in our family forever. It was the only pan we used to make shortbread, and I'm pretty sure my mum still uses it today. This simple recipe uses only four ingredients, and if you use pure Irish butter, you'll be rewarded with one of the best shortbreads you've ever tasted.

1   Preheat the oven to 300°F (150°C). Grease an 8-inch square baking pan and line it with parchment paper.

2   In a large bowl, cream together the butter and sugar with a wooden spoon until pale, light, and fluffy.

3   Add the flour and cornstarch. Mix very lightly until you have a smooth dough.

4   Press the dough into the prepared pan. With a knife, cut the dough into sixteen fingers measuring 1 x 4 inches (these marks will make it easier to cut your baked shortbread). Prick the dough all over with a fork.

5   Bake for about 50 minutes, until golden brown. Let the shortbread cool slightly in the pan, then, while it's still warm, cut along the marks into 16 bars.

6   Store the shortbread in an airtight container at room temperature for up to 4 days.

BUTTER **WHIRL BISCUITS**

MAKES 12 TO
14 COOKIES

¾ cup (1½ sticks/
170 grams) butter,
softened

½ cup (57 grams)
confectioners' sugar

½ teaspoon pure
vanilla extract

1¼ cups (170 grams)
all-purpose flour

6 or 7 maraschino
cherries, halved

NOTE

If you don't have
a piping bag, you
can use a zip-top
plastic bag instead.
Transfer the dough
to the bag and
cut the tip off one
corner for piping.
Just make sure the
plastic is strong, or
the bag might burst
while you're piping
the cookies.

Maraschino cherries proudly sit upon swirls of buttery piped dough in this cookie, the likes of which are found all over Ireland. They might be homemade like they were in my house (and as is my preference, of course) or store-bought, but either way, they feature a wonderful crumbly texture that goes really well with the chewy cherries. It's not uncommon to sandwich two cookies with jam—or even better, try sandwiching them with Best-Ever Buttercream Frosting (page 276) if you want to get really indulgent. Cookies this pretty are nice to give as a gift—arrange them in a decorative cookie tin and finish it off with a colorful ribbon.

1 Preheat the oven to 325°F (165°C). Line a cookie sheet with parchment paper.

2 In a large bowl, cream together the butter, sugar, and vanilla with a wooden spoon until fluffy and pale in color.

3 Add the flour and stir until well combined.

4 Transfer the dough to a piping bag fitted with a large star tip.

5 Pipe the dough into 12 to 14 flat whirls on your prepared cookie sheet. Put a cherry half on each one.

6 Bake for 18 to 20 minutes, until pale gold. Leave to cool on the cookie sheet for 5 minutes, then transfer to a wire rack.

7 Store the biscuits in an airtight container at room temperature for up to 3 days.

SIMPLEST BUTTERY
VIENNESE FINGERS

**MAKES 9 OR 10
SANDWICH COOKIES**

1 cup (2 sticks/
225 grams) butter,
softened

⅔ cup (76 grams)
confectioners' sugar,
sifted

4 large egg yolks

2 teaspoons pure vanilla
extract

2 cups (284 grams)
all-purpose flour

1 cup (6 ounces/
170 grams) chopped
bittersweet chocolate

Vanilla Buttercream
Frosting (page 276)

When I was a child, I was enchanted by the Viennese Fingers I saw in bakeries: buttery cookies edged with chocolate and filled with creamy frosting. They were so elegant and pretty to me—a special-occasion kind of cookie. But rather than buying them, I decided to go home and try baking them myself. I piped the dough into longish finger shapes, dipped both ends of the baked cookies into melted chocolate, and sandwiched them with a thick layer of my Vanilla Buttercream Frosting, and they came out just like the ones I saw at the bakery. The buttercream can be optional if you'd like a cookie that's a little less rich.

1   Preheat the oven to 350°F (180°C). Line a cookie sheet with parchment paper.

2   In a large bowl, cream together the butter and confectioners' sugar with a wooden spoon until fluffy and pale in color.

3   Add the egg yolks and vanilla and mix until combined.

4   Add the flour and stir until the mixture is smooth. Spoon the dough into a piping bag fitted with a large star tip.

5   Pipe the dough into 18 to 20 wavy 3-inch lengths on the prepared cookie sheet.

6   Bake for about 12 minutes, until the cookies are light golden and crisp. Transfer to a wire rack to cool completely.

RECIPE CONTINUES

7   While the cookies are cooling, melt the chocolate in a
small heatproof bowl in the microwave or over a bain-
marie (see page 30).

8   Dip the ends of each cookie in the melted chocolate
and place them on a sheet of parchment. Let sit for about
1 hour, until the chocolate has set.

9   Put the buttercream in a piping bag fitted with a large star
tip. Pipe a line of buttercream over the flat side of a cookie
and then sandwich it together with another. Repeat with
the remaining cookies.

10   Store the cookies in an airtight container at room
temperature for up to 3 days.

NEW ZEALAND **AFGHAN COOKIES**

⅔ cup (142 grams) butter, softened

⅓ cup (57 grams) light brown sugar

1 large egg

1 teaspoon pure vanilla extract

1 cup (142 grams) all-purpose flour

2 tablespoons unsweetened cocoa powder

⅓ cup (57 grams) unsweetened shredded coconut

1½ cups (64 grams) cornflakes, lightly crushed

½ cup (3 ounces/ 85 grams) chopped milk chocolate

The very first cookbook I used when I was a child was loaded with cookie and bar recipes. My mum gave it to me (who knows where she found it), and it was perfect because every recipe was so easy to make. I pretty much baked everything in the book, many of them multiple times. I can still remember baking in the evening in the quiet kitchen. I would weigh all the ingredients, referring to the cookbook lying open on the counter, covered with flour. The secret in this recipe is adding cornflakes, which gives the cookies a nice crunch. I love them as much today as I did the very first time I made them.

1 Preheat the oven to 350°F (180°C) and line a cookie sheet with parchment paper.

2 In a large bowl, cream together the butter and sugar with a wooden spoon until soft and light in color.

3 Add in the egg and vanilla and mix until combined.

4 Gently stir in the flour, cocoa powder, coconut, and cornflakes and mix until incorporated.

5 Using a tablespoon measure, scoop out heaping tablespoons of the dough, roll them into balls, and place them on the prepared cookie sheet. Leave some space between the cookies, as they'll spread during baking.

6 Bake for 10 to 12 minutes, until lightly golden. Transfer the cookies to a wire rack to cool.

RECIPE CONTINUES

7   While the cookies are cooling, melt the milk chocolate in a small heatproof bowl in the microwave or over a bain-marie (see page 30).

8   Set the wire rack with the cookies over a sheet of parchment paper. Dip half of each cooled cookie into the melted chocolate, then return it to the rack and let set at room temperature for about 1 hour, until the chocolate has hardened.

9   Store the cookies in an airtight container at room temperature for up to 3 days.

CORNISH FAIRINGS BISCUITS

MAKES 18 COOKIES

1½ cups (213 grams) all-purpose flour

½ cup (85 grams) light brown sugar

2 teaspoons ground ginger

2 teaspoons baking powder

1 teaspoon baking soda

1 teaspoon ground cinnamon

½ teaspoon salt

½ cup (1 stick/ 115 grams) butter, chilled and diced

6 tablespoons (90 milliliters) golden syrup

In Ireland, biscuits made with a few simple, quality ingredients are quite popular, which is why this recipe is so beloved there. Crinkly and soft, the Cornish Fairings Biscuit is said to originate in Cornwall, England, and I remember baking and eating them myself for much of my youth. Here cinnamon and ginger offer up a little warmth, while the golden syrup gives each bite a very pleasant chewiness. I can't think of another cookie that pairs so nicely with an afternoon cup of tea on a chilly day.

1   Preheat the oven to 400°F (200°C) and line two cookie sheets with parchment paper.

2   In a large bowl, stir together the flour, brown sugar, ginger, baking powder, baking soda, cinnamon, and salt with a wooden spoon.

3   Add the butter and, using your fingertips, rub it into the dry ingredients until the mixture resembles coarse bread crumbs.

4   Stir in the golden syrup to form a firm dough.

5   Using a tablespoon measure, scoop out level tablespoons of the dough, roll them into balls, and place them on the prepared cookie sheets. Leave some space between the biscuits, as they'll spread a bit during baking.

6   Bake for 7 to 8 minutes, until golden brown. Let cool on the cookie sheets for a few minutes before transferring to a wire rack.

7   Store the biscuits in an airtight container at room temperature for up to 3 days.

AUSTRALIAN ANZAC COOKIES

MAKES 28 COOKIES

1 cup (142 grams)
all-purpose flour

⅔ cup (142 grams) sugar

1 cup (85 grams)
rolled oats

1 cup (85 grams)
unsweetened shredded
coconut

½ cup (1 stick/
115 grams) butter

¼ cup (71 milliliters)
golden syrup

½ teaspoon baking soda

1 tablespoon boiling
water

The Australian and New Zealand Army Corps (Anzac) was formed during World War I; these cookies were often sent to Anzac soldiers stationed overseas because they could be transported without crumbling to pieces and the ingredients didn't spoil easily. But the real reason for their popularity is that they taste great. I like them because they have a nice crunch and I usually have all the ingredients in my pantry.

1 Preheat the oven to 350°F (180°C) and line two cookie sheets with parchment paper.

2 In a large bowl, mix together the flour, sugar, oats, and coconut. Make a well in the center with your wooden spoon.

3 In a separate bowl, combine the butter and golden syrup in a medium heatproof bowl and melt them together in the microwave or over a bain-marie (see page 30). Set aside.

4 In a small bowl, dissolve the baking soda in the boiling water to activate it. It will foam up instantly. Immediately add it to the butter mixture.

5 Add the butter mixture to the dry ingredients and stir until well combined.

6 Using a tablespoon measure, scoop out level tablespoons of the dough, roll them into balls, and place them on the prepared cookie sheets. Flatten each ball gently with your fingers. Leave some space between the cookies, as they'll spread during baking.

7 Bake for 10 to 12 minutes, until golden brown. Transfer the cookies to a wire rack to cool.

8 Store the cookies in an airtight container at room temperature for up to 3 days.

OLD-FASHIONED GINGERNUTS

MAKES 28 COOKIES

2 ⅓ cups (325 grams) self-rising flour (see page 304)

1 cup (170 grams) light brown sugar

1 tablespoon ground ginger

1 teaspoon baking soda

½ cup (1 stick/ 115 grams) butter

¼ cup (71 milliliters) golden syrup

1 large egg, beaten

When I was growing up, these crunchy cookies were commonly known as gingernuts, but they may be more familiar to you as gingersnaps. They go hand in hand with a cup of coffee and are great for dunking. When I was a chef at a law firm in Dublin, every morning I would get an order sheet listing which cookies should go in each meeting room. Gingernuts were on the list for every room, every day.

1 Preheat the oven to 325°F (165°C) and line two cookie sheets with parchment paper.

2 Sift together the flour, brown sugar, ginger, and baking soda into a large bowl.

3 Put the butter and golden syrup in a medium heatproof bowl and melt them together in the microwave or over a bain-marie (see page 30). Stir to combine and set aside to cool slightly.

4 Pour the cooled butter mixture over the dry ingredients and stir with a wooden spoon to combine.

5 Add the egg and mix thoroughly.

6 Scoop the dough into walnut-size balls (roughly 1 tablespoon each) and place them on the prepared cookie sheets. Press down on the balls to flatten them slightly. Leave some space between the cookies, as they'll spread during baking.

7 Bake for 12 minutes, or until golden brown. Transfer to a wire rack to cool completely.

8 Store the cookies in an airtight container at room temperature for up to 3 days.

FIVE-INGREDIENT COCONUT KISSES

MAKES 30 COOKIES

¾ cup (1½ sticks/ 170 grams) butter, softened

2 cups (225 grams) confectioners' sugar

3 large egg whites

1 cup (142 grams) all-purpose flour

2⅔ cups (8 ounces/ 225 grams) unsweetened shredded coconut

For a time, I was a chef at a law firm in Dublin. The chef I replaced there was kind enough to hand down the recipe for these cookies. They are much like a macaroon, with a browned outside and chewy, coconutty inside, and the lawyers loved them, as did I. Eventually I left that position, moved to the US, worked at several other jobs . . . Ten years went by, and I lost track of the recipe. Until one day I was flicking through my recipe notebook and found it tucked in among the pages. You can imagine how happy I was to rediscover these kisses and to be able to share them with you here.

1   Preheat the oven to 350°F (180°C) and line two cookie sheets with parchment paper.

2   In a large bowl, cream together the butter and confectioners' sugar with a wooden spoon until soft and light in color.

3   Add the egg whites and mix until combined.

4   Fold in the flour and the coconut.

5   Using a tablespoon measure, scoop out heaping tablespoons of the dough, roll them into balls, and place them on the prepared cookie sheets. Leave some space between the cookies, as they'll spread during baking.

6   Bake for 12 to 13 minutes, until very light golden brown. Transfer the cookies to a wire rack to cool.

7   Store the cookies in an airtight container at room temperature for up to 3 days.

SIMPLIFIED CHOCOLATE & HAZELNUT COOKIES

MAKES 35 COOKIES

⅔ cup (142 grams) butter, softened

⅔ cup (142 grams) granulated sugar

⅓ cup (57 grams) light brown sugar

2 large eggs

2 teaspoons pure vanilla extract

2 cups (283 grams) all-purpose flour

1 teaspoon baking powder

1 teaspoon salt

1⅓ cups (8 ounces/ 225 grams) chopped bittersweet chocolate

1 cup (142 grams) hazelnuts, chopped

Wexford is the town in southeast Ireland where I grew up. It's also where I found one of the first jobs I ever had, working at an upscale spa. Although the spa was considered a healthy retreat, everywhere you turned there were cookies. They served them at every meal. They served them with coffee or tea. You could get a cookie any time you wanted one. The spa patrons raved about these, probably because they're loaded with chocolate chips. Be sure to use the highest quality bittersweet chocolate chips you can find—it's a big part of what makes these so good.

1 Preheat the oven to 350°F (180°C) and line two cookie sheets with parchment paper.

2 In a large bowl, cream together the butter and sugars with a wooden spoon until soft and light in color.

3 Add the eggs one at a time, followed by the vanilla and mix until combined.

4 Stir in the flour, baking powder, and salt and then the chocolate and hazelnuts. Mix until everything is well combined.

5 Cover and refrigerate the dough for 1 hour (this makes it much easier to scoop).

RECIPE CONTINUES

6 Using a tablespoon measure, scoop out heaping tablespoons of the dough, roll them into balls, and place them on the prepared cookie sheets. Press down on the balls to flatten them slightly. Leave some space between the cookies, as they'll spread during baking.

7 Bake for 12 to 15 minutes, until golden brown. Transfer to a wire rack to cool.

8 Store the cookies in an airtight container at room temperature for up to 4 days.

5-STAR CHOCOLATE CHIP COOKIES

MAKES 30 COOKIES

1 cup (2 sticks/ 225 grams) butter, softened

¾ cup (170 grams) granulated sugar

1 cup (170 grams) dark brown sugar

2 large eggs

2⅔ cups (368 grams) all-purpose flour

1¼ teaspoons baking soda

1 teaspoon salt

2⅓ cups (14 ounces/ 396 grams) chopped bittersweet chocolate

NOTE

I prefer to use a really good-quality bittersweet chocolate bar rather than chocolate chips for this recipe. That richness of the chocolate takes these cookies to another level.

In San Francisco I was thrilled to work as pastry chef at a high-end restaurant. Every day I would get up at the crack of dawn to mix up dough and freeze ice cream for desserts as exquisite as the rest of the Michelin-starred dinner menu. One of my specialties was this chocolate chip cookie. We used only Valrhona chocolate, and those cookies were huge—we used an ice cream scoop to measure the dough onto the baking sheets. The cookies were usually stacked high at the front of the restaurant where anyone could come in and buy them to take home. Often, one person would buy all of them, and I'd need to bake more in a big hurry. My version encourages you to make them a bit smaller, though you should definitely try them with a good-quality bittersweet chocolate.

1   Preheat the oven to 375°F (190°C) and line two cookie sheets with parchment paper.

2   In a large bowl, cream together the butter and sugars with a wooden spoon until soft and light in color.

3   Slowly mix the eggs one by one into the butter-sugar mixture.

4   In a separate bowl, mix together the flour, baking soda, and salt.

5   Add the dry ingredients to the wet ingredients and mix until combined. Fold in the chopped chocolate. Chill the dough for 30 minutes.

RECIPE CONTINUES

6　Using a tablespoon measure, scoop out big, heaping tablespoons of the dough, roll them into balls, and place them on the prepared cookie sheets. Leave some space between the cookies, as they'll spread during baking.

7　Bake for 10 to 12 minutes. Be careful not to overbake; you want the cookies soft in the center and chewy on the outside.

8　Transfer the cookies to a wire rack to cool.

9　These cookies are best enjoyed straight out of the oven, but if you have leftovers, store the cooled cookies in an airtight container at room temperature for up to 3 days.

TRIPLE CHOCOLATE CHIP COOKIES

MAKES 37 COOKIES

1 cup (6 ounces/ 170 grams) chopped bittersweet chocolate

¾ cup (1½ sticks/ 170 grams) butter, softened

¾ cup (170 grams) granulated sugar

⅔ cup (115 grams) dark brown sugar

1 tablespoon molasses

3 large eggs

2 cups (284 grams) all-purpose flour

½ cup (57 grams) unsweetened cocoa powder

1 teaspoon baking soda

1 teaspoon salt

1½ cups (9 ounces/ 255 grams) milk chocolate chips

This is really a brownie masquerading as a cookie, with a dark, dense, fudgy interior. I made these when I worked at a restaurant in San Francisco. My day would always start incredibly early, so by 5:30 a.m. I would have baking sheets lined with mounds of triple chocolate chip cookie dough ready to slide into the oven. With lots of bittersweet chocolate, cocoa powder, and milk chocolate chips, these cookies are a true triple threat, and they were always practically irresistible to me. At nine a.m., I'd be so hungry for breakfast that it would take all my willpower *not* to eat them. On my last day at that restaurant, I gave in and ate two of them right out of the oven, slowly savoring every bite.

1 Preheat the oven to 350°F (180°C) and line two cookie sheets with parchment paper.

2 Melt the chocolate in a small heatproof bowl in the microwave or over a bain-marie. (see page 30). Set aside to cool for 10 minutes.

3 In a large bowl, cream together the butter and sugars with a wooden spoon until soft and light in color.

4 Slowly stir in the molasses and melted chocolate.

5 Add the eggs one at a time and mix until well combined.

6 Sift the flour, cocoa powder, baking soda, and salt into the bowl and mix until the dough comes together.

7 Fold in the chocolate chips until evenly distributed.

RECIPE CONTINUES

8   Using a tablespoon measure, scoop out heaping tablespoons of the dough, roll them into balls, and place them on the prepared cookie sheets. Leave some space between the cookies, as they'll spread during baking.

9   Bake for 8 to 10 minutes. Don't be tempted to bake the cookies for longer than this—when they're perfectly baked, they are like a brownie on the inside. Transfer to a wire rack to cool.

10 Store the cookies in an airtight container at room temperature for up to 3 days.

TAHOE'S LAYERED
PEANUT BUTTER BARS

MAKES 24 BARS

1½ cups (3 sticks/
340 grams) butter,
softened

1 cup (225 grams) sugar

1 cup (225 grams)
smooth peanut butter

1 large egg

1 teaspoon pure vanilla
extract

1 teaspoon salt

2 cups (283 grams)
all-purpose flour

2⅓ cups (198 grams)
unsweetened shredded
coconut

1 cup (142 grams)
salted roasted peanuts,
chopped

2 cups (12 ounces/
340 grams) chopped
milk chocolate

Lake Tahoe, a ski resort and gambling destination straddling the border between California and Nevada, was not my first choice of places to live when I left Ireland, but a bakery in one of the casinos there offered me a job, and I grabbed it. At the bakery, I was required to start work at the shocking hour of three a.m. When it's that early, it's hard to know what an appropriate breakfast is, so I'd often eat one of the bakery's peanut butter bars, which featured a layer of chocolate and were salty and sweet and really very good. As time went by, the number of bars I ate each day started to climb, and I realized I had to limit my peanut butter bar intake or risk a slippery slide into gluttony. Consider yourself warned.

1   Preheat the oven to 350°F (180°C) and line a 9 x 13-inch baking pan with parchment paper.

2   In a large bowl, cream together the butter and sugar with a wooden spoon until light and fluffy.

3   Mix in the peanut butter, followed by the egg and vanilla.

4   Add the salt, flour, and coconut and mix until well combined.

5   Spread the mixture evenly in the prepared pan.

6   Scatter the peanuts over the top. Press them into the dough with your hand.

RECIPE CONTINUES

7   Bake for 25 to 30 minutes, until golden brown on top. Let cool in the pan for 20 minutes.

8   Melt the chocolate in a small heatproof bowl in the microwave or over a bain-marie (see page 30). Spread a thin layer of the melted chocolate over the top of the bars in the pan. Transfer the pan to the fridge and let the chocolate for 2 hours. When the chocolate has set, cut into 24 bars.

9   Store the bars in an airtight container in the fridge for up to 5 days.

COCONUT & JAM SQUARES

MAKES 16 SQUARES

FOR THE SHORTBREAD BASE

1½ cups (213 grams) all-purpose flour

⅔ cup (142 grams) butter, softened

½ cup (57 grams) confectioners' sugar

FOR THE COCONUT TOPPING

2 large eggs, at room temperature

⅓ cup (71 grams) sugar

2 cups (6 ounces/ 170 grams) unsweetened shredded coconut

⅔ cup (225 grams) raspberry jam

The buttery shortbread base, layer of jam—raspberry is my flavor of choice—and luscious coconut top of these squares are all very tempting. One of the things I like most about this recipe is a fringe benefit I discovered after they were baked: the sides of the block are trimmed before it's cut into squares, leaving odds and ends that beg to be eaten—by the baker, of course.

1   Preheat the oven to 350°F (180°C). Grease an 8-inch square cake pan and line it with parchment paper.

2   *To make the shortbread:* Place the flour, butter, and sugar in a large bowl.

3   Rub the butter into the dry ingredients with your fingers until it forms a loose dough. Press the dough into the prepared pan.

4   Bake for about 15 minutes, until just golden. Set aside to cool while you make the topping. Leave the oven on.

5   *To make the topping:* In a medium bowl, whisk together the eggs and sugar for 3 to 4 minutes, until light, fluffy, and thickened. Stir in the coconut.

6   Spread the jam evenly over the cooled shortbread base, followed by the coconut topping. Press down on the topping with the back of a spoon to even it out.

7   Bake for 20 minutes, or until golden brown on top. Let cool in the pan on a wire rack.

8   Cut the block into 2-inch squares (trim the edges first for neater squares, if you'd like).

9   Store the squares in an airtight container at room temperature for up to 3 days.

IRISH **RHUBARB CRUMBLE**

MAKES 5 OR 6 SERVINGS

8 cups (2 pounds/ 900 grams) chopped rhubarb (1-inch pieces)

⅓ cup plus ¼ cup (128 grams) sugar

1¼ cups (170 grams) all-purpose flour

6 tablespoons (¾ stick/85 grams) butter, cold, cut into cubes

Whipped cream, for serving

Imagine a seven-year-old Gemma, standing at the kitchen table rubbing butter and sugar between her fingers to make a topping for her mum's rhubarb crumble. This was a very familiar scene in my youth, and as a quintessential Irish dessert, it was one of the first recipes my mum taught me. It's so simple—you only need to cut up rhubarb and toss it with a little sugar. The sugar tames the tang of the rhubarb and the topping develops a nice crunchy, crumbly texture when it's baked. After a recent visit back home, I noticed my mum still had the dish we always used to make this, and thanks to her, I'm now the proud owner of a well-worn, very retro Pyrex baking dish.

1   Preheat the oven to 400°F (200°C).

2   Put the rhubarb in a 9-inch baking dish. Add ⅓ cup (71 grams) of the sugar and stir to coat the rhubarb.

3   In a medium bowl, combine the flour and butter and, using your fingertips, rub the butter into the flour until the mixture resembles coarse bread crumbs.

4   Add the remaining ¼ cup (57 grams) sugar and stir to combine.

5   Spoon the crumble over the rhubarb in the baking dish and spread it out until the surface is even. Do not press the crumble down hard.

6   Bake for 40 to 45 minutes, until the top is browned and the rhubarb filling is bubbling.

7   Serve hot, with whipped cream. Store leftovers in the fridge, covered, for up to 3 days.

MY ALL-AMERICAN
APPLE & BLUEBERRY COBBLER

MAKES 6 TO 8 SERVINGS

FOR THE FILLING

4 apples (Granny Smith or Bramley), peeled, cored, and chopped (about 4 cups/455 grams)

1 cup (142 grams) blueberries

2 tablespoons sugar

1 teaspoon pure vanilla extract

FOR THE COBBLER TOPPING

1 cup (142 grams) all-purpose flour

1 cup (225 grams) sugar

¼ teaspoon salt

½ cup (1 stick/ 115 grams) butter, cubed, softened

1 large egg, beaten

Vanilla ice cream, for serving

When I was a chef at a tech company in the San Francisco Bay area, this was one of the "breakfasts" I'd make to entice the engineers to come to work earlier in the morning. It's really more of a dessert, a cobbler loaded with fruit, dolloped with a biscuit batter, and baked until warm and bubbling. This version features tart, crisp apples mixed with fresh blueberries. Some people might not consider it a true breakfast, but I didn't get any complaints. And the engineers started coming to work on time.

1   Preheat the oven to 350°F (180°C).

2   *To make the filling:* In a large bowl, mix together the apples, blueberries, sugar, and vanilla. Spread the fruit mixture in the bottom of an 8-inch square baking dish.

3   *To make the topping:* In a large bowl, stir together the flour, sugar, and salt.

4   Add the butter and, using your fingertips, rub it into the dry ingredients until the mixture resembles coarse bread crumbs.

5   Add the egg and stir to combine.

6   Spoon the topping over the fruit. There might be some gaps, but don't worry—the topping will spread out as it bakes.

7   Bake for 45 to 55 minutes, until the topping is golden brown and the fruit filling is bubbling.

8   Serve the cobbler warm, with vanilla ice cream. Store leftovers in the fridge, covered, for up to 3 days.

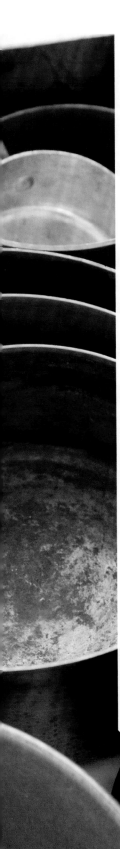

Chapter 2

POTS & PANS

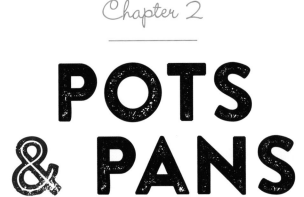

I SOMETIMES FORGET THAT MANY "BAKING" RECIPES actually start in a pot on the stove, not in the oven—but some of my fondest food memories are of my mum making "stovetop" desserts like crepes or crème brûlée. When I make them now, they always transport me back to my childhood home in Ireland. Some of the recipes I like best are cooked entirely on the stovetop, like Creamy Rice Pudding (page 103) or Silky-Smooth Chocolate Soup (page 100). Others are started on the stovetop and then finished in the oven, like Dinner Party Chocolate Profiteroles (page 121), or sent to the freezer, like Coconut Semifreddo with Tropical Fruit Salsa (page 113). You'll find that the treats in this chapter are often creamy or luscious and rich and are sophisticated enough to serve to company. But they are homey enough that families will love them, too, particularly recipes like Christopher's Buttermilk Pancakes (page 87).

MUM'S PANCAKE TUESDAY CREPES

¾ cup (115 grams)
all-purpose flour

¼ teaspoon salt

1 large egg

1¼ cups (282 milliliters)
whole milk

1 tablespoon (15 grams)
butter, melted, plus
more butter for cooking

¼ cup (57 grams) sugar,
for serving

Juice of 1 lemon, for
serving

In Ireland, Shrove Tuesday—the day before Ash Wednesday—is known as Pancake Tuesday. It is common in Irish Catholic households to eat pancakes for dinner on that day (and when I say pancakes, I actually mean crepes, which we call pancakes in Ireland). At our house, the kids would line up in the kitchen, each of us holding a plate, while my mum would make crepes to order. As each crepe finished cooking, she would sprinkle it with sugar and lemon juice, fold it in half and then in half again, and place it on the plate of whoever was first in line. The lucky recipient would eagerly eat it and quickly get back in line to get another.

1   In a large bowl, combine the flour and salt and make a well in the center.

2   Crack the egg into the middle. Pour in the milk and start whisking from the center, gradually drawing the flour into the egg and milk. Once all the flour is incorporated, whisk until smooth. Add the melted butter and whisk to combine.

3   Cover and refrigerate the batter for at least 30 minutes. (This is an important step, as bubbles develop in the batter as it rests.)

4   When you're ready to cook the crepes, heat a large skillet over medium heat. Melt a little butter in the pan to keep the crepes from sticking.

5   Ladle some batter (roughly $1/3$ cup/71 milliliters) into the skillet, tilting the pan to coat the bottom with a thin, even layer, then let the crepe cook, undisturbed. If the pan is at the right temperature, the crepe should turn golden underneath after about 45 seconds and will be ready to turn.

6   Ease a long, thin spatula under the crepe, then quickly lift and flip it over. Make sure the crepe is lying flat against bottom of the pan with no folds, then cook for 30 seconds to 1 minute, until golden brown on the second side. Turn the crepe out onto a plate. Repeat to cook the remaining batter, adding butter to the pan between crepes as needed.

7   To serve, simply dust the crepes with some sugar, squeeze over some fresh lemon juice, and enjoy warm. Store any leftover crepes in the fridge, covered, for up to 2 days.

CHRISTOPHER'S BUTTERMILK PANCAKES

MAKES 5 OR 6 SERVINGS

4 tablespoons (½ stick/57 grams) butter, plus more for cooking and serving

2 cups (282 grams) all-purpose flour

2 teaspoons baking powder

1 teaspoon baking soda

3 tablespoons sugar

1 teaspoon salt

2 cups (480 milliliters) buttermilk

2 large eggs

1 teaspoon pure vanilla extract

Maple syrup, for serving

To make some extra money when I was living in San Francisco, I took a second job taking care of a local couple's daughter. Once, they asked me to come to their weekend home in Napa to watch their daughter and to cook breakfast. The husband, Christopher, gave me his recipe for pancakes—a family favorite. I doubled the recipe to ensure there would be enough for everyone. As I flipped them on the griddle, I could see why everyone loved the recipe—they were the thickest, fluffiest pancakes I had ever made. I placed the plate on the dining table, stacked high with a tower of pancakes, and they were amazed. What happened? they asked. Why are they like this? Turns out, I had accidentally doubled the baking powder and baking soda—the leavening ingredients—which is a baking no-no and usually results in disaster, but in this case, led to pancake perfection. I never told them what I had done . . .

1 Melt the butter and set aside to cool.

2 Mix together the flour, baking powder, baking soda, sugar, and salt in a large bowl.

3 In a large measuring cup or medium bowl, whisk together the buttermilk, eggs, and vanilla.

4 Pour the wet ingredients into the dry ingredients and lightly whisk to combine. Lumps are okay; resist the urge to mix more. (The secret to thick, fluffy pancakes is not to overmix. My trick is to stir it enough times to spell

RECIPE CONTINUES

P-A-N-C-A-K-E, and then stop.) Add the melted butter and stir briefly just to combine.

5   Heat a large nonstick skillet over medium-low heat. Melt some butter in the skillet to keep the pancakes from sticking.

6   Spoon a big spoonful (roughly ⅓ cup/71 milliliters) of batter into the pan for each pancake. Cook for about 4 minutes on the first side, until you see bubbles form and then pop on the top of the pancake. (Forming bubbles on top is really important, because they hold the pancake up and keep it thick—I call them pancake pillars.) Flip the pancakes and cook for about 2 minutes on the second side, until brown. Transfer the pancakes to a plate and repeat with the remaining batter, adding butter to the skillet as needed between batches.

7   Enjoy warm, with butter and maple syrup. Any leftovers can be stored covered in the fridge, covered, for up to 2 days. To reheat, cover with aluminum foil and warm in a preheated 300°F (180°C) oven for 10 minutes.

MY FAMOUS RED VELVET PANCAKES WITH CREAM CHEESE FROSTING

MAKES 5 OR 6 SERVINGS

FOR THE CREAM CHEESE FROSTING

½ cup (4 ounces/ 115 grams) cream cheese, softened

1 teaspoon pure vanilla extract

2 tablespoons sugar

¼ cup (57milliliters) heavy cream

FOR THE RED VELVET PANCAKES

1¾ cups (247 grams) all-purpose flour

3 tablespoons sugar

2 tablespoons unsweetened cocoa powder

1 teaspoon ground cinnamon

1 teaspoon salt

1½ teaspoons baking powder

½ teaspoon baking soda

1¼ cups (282 milliliters) buttermilk

2 large eggs

1 teaspoon pure vanilla extract

When I was making breakfasts for a Silicon Valley tech company, I was always trying to lure the engineers into the office earlier on Fridays, the hardest day to get those guys to work on time. One day I thought, *Everyone goes crazy over red velvet cake—what if I made red velvet pancakes?* So on the next Friday, that's what I gave them: big, soft, fluffy red velvet pancakes, dolloped with a cream cheese frosting and drizzled with maple syrup. I became an instant legend, and those pancakes became the regular Friday breakfast. Word got out quickly—no one wanted to miss breakfast that day—and attendance improved dramatically. In fact, sometimes people who didn't even work there would show up to eat.

1 *To make the cream cheese frosting:* In a medium bowl, whisk together the cream cheese, vanilla, and sugar until smooth.

2 Add the cream and whisk for about 2 minutes, until the frosting thickens. Cover and refrigerate until ready to use.

3 *To make the red velvet pancakes:* Sift together the flour, sugar, cocoa powder, cinnamon, salt, baking powder, and baking soda into a large bowl.

4 In a measuring cup, mix together the buttermilk, eggs, vanilla, and food coloring.

5 Add the buttermilk mixture to the dry ingredients and stir until mostly combined. Gently fold in the melted butter, being careful not to overmix. The batter will be very thick, but that's okay. Refrigerate the batter for 15 minutes.

RECIPE AND INGREDIENTS CONTINUE

1 tablespoon red food coloring

¼ cup (57 grams) butter, melted and cooled, plus more for cooking

Maple syrup, for serving

6   Heat a large nonstick skillet over medium-low heat. Brush the pan with a little butter to keep the pancakes from sticking.

7   Spoon a big spoonful (roughly ⅓ cup/71 milliliters) of the batter into the pan for each pancake. Cook for about 4 minutes on the first side, until the pancakes puff up, the tops are full of bubbles, and the edges begin to look dry. Flip the pancakes and cook for about 2 minutes, until lightly golden on the second side. Transfer the pancakes to a plate and repeat with the remaining batter, adding butter to the skillet as needed between batches.

8   Serve the finished pancakes hot, topped with a big dollop of the frosting and drizzled with maple syrup. Any leftovers can be stored in the fridge, covered, for up to 2 days. To reheat, cover with aluminum foil and warm in a preheated 300°F (180°C) oven for 10 minutes.

EGGY BREAD
LIKE MUM USED TO MAKE

MAKES 4 SERVINGS

4 tablespoons (½ stick/57 grams) butter, softened, plus more for cooking

4 thick slices white sandwich bread

3 large eggs

3 tablespoons sugar, for sprinkling

Another treat my mum used to make when I was growing up was eggy bread, also known as French toast to Americans or *pain perdu* ("lost bread") to the French. It's a practical recipe because it uses ordinary pantry ingredients—bread, eggs, butter, sugar—and yet as I child, I saw it as a kind of culinary sorcery. I couldn't believe my mum could turn such unpromising ingredients into something that tasted so good. She would sprinkle the hot bread with sugar and we would eat it while it was still warm. She continues to make the same magic today for my niece and nephews.

1 Butter the slices of bread on both sides.

2 In a shallow dish, whisk the eggs.

3 Heat a large skillet over medium-low heat. Brush the skillet with some butter. Line a plate with paper towels and set it nearby.

4 Place the bread in the egg and let soak for 3 minutes. Turn the slices over and let soak on the other side for 3 minutes.

5 One at a time, lift the bread out of the egg, letting any extra egg drain back into the dish, and place the bread in the hot skillet. Fry for about 3 minutes on each side, until the bread is crisp and golden brown on both sides. Transfer the eggy bread to the paper towel–lined plate and sprinkle generously with sugar on both sides.

6 Enjoy while still warm. Store any leftovers in the fridge, covered, for up to 24 hours. To reheat, cover with aluminum foil and warm in a preheated 300°F (180°C) oven for 10 minutes.

CHOCOLATE
BREAD & BUTTER PUDDING

1½ cups (340 milliliters) heavy cream

¾ cup (4.5 ounces/ 128 grams) chopped bittersweet chocolate

½ cup (115 milliliters) whole milk

6 large egg yolks

½ cup (115 grams) sugar

2 teaspoons pure vanilla extract

1 teaspoon salt

4 tablespoons (½ stick/ 57 grams) butter, softened

10 to 13 slices white sandwich bread

Vanilla ice cream, for serving

Bread-and-butter pudding is so dangerously addictive! I used to make this at a restaurant in San Francisco by soaking slices of homemade brioche in a creamy custard made with fine melted dark chocolate, cream, and egg yolks. It was so rich, it was practically sinful. It was baked in a rectangular pan but I would cut out circular pieces with a cookie cutter to create a beautiful plated dessert that the patrons would appreciate. This left bread pudding scraps that seemed a shame to throw away, so I would collect them into a big bowl for the staff to enjoy. I consciously tried to keep from eating those scraps myself. It was a war between self-control and self-indulgence, a fight I didn't always win.

1   In a medium saucepan, combine the cream, chocolate, and milk and heat over medium heat just until the chocolate has melted. Remove from the heat and set aside to cool.

2   In a large bowl, whisk the egg yolks with the sugar until combined.

3   While whisking swiftly, gradually pour the cooled chocolate mixture into the egg mixture.

4   Strain the custard through a fine-mesh sieve into a large bowl to remove any lumps.

5   Whisk in the vanilla and salt. Set aside to cool completely, about 1 hour.

6   Butter the slices of bread. Remove and discard the crusts and cut the buttered bread into cubes.

RECIPE CONTINUES

7   Add the bread to the bowl with the custard, pushing the bread down with a spatula until submerged. Cover and refrigerate for at least 20 minutes and up to overnight for the bread to soak up the custard. (I usually let it soak overnight.)

8   When you are ready to bake, preheat the oven to 325°F (165°C). Butter an 8-inch square baking dish.

9   Pour your bread pudding mixture into the prepared baking dish.

10 Bake for 30 to 35 minutes. It's okay if the bread pudding is a little soft in the middle when it comes out of the oven— that means it is nice and saucy on the inside.

11 Serve warm, with vanilla ice cream. Store any leftovers in the fridge, covered, for up to 3 days.

DARK CHOCOLATE & HAZELNUT PÂTÉ

MAKES 8 SERVINGS

1½ cups (213 grams) hazelnuts

1⅔ cups (10 ounces/ 285 grams) chopped bittersweet chocolate

2 tablespoons (28 grams) butter

1¾ cups (395 milliliters) heavy cream

4 large egg yolks

¼ cup (57 grams) sugar

½ teaspoon salt

Whipped cream, for serving

This is an impressive dessert to share at a dinner party—a sweet twist on the classic savory appetizer. Here bittersweet chocolate and roughly chopped hazelnuts are molded in a loaf pan. After a good long chill in the fridge, the "pâté" is sliced and topped with dollops of whipped cream. It's a lovely balance of nuts and chocolate, smooth and crunchy.

1   Preheat the oven to 350°F (180°C).

2   Place the hazelnuts on a baking sheet and toast in the oven for 15 to 20 minutes, until golden brown. Place the warm hazelnuts in a clean dish towel and rub vigorously to remove their skins.

3   Transfer the hazelnuts to a food processor and pulse for about 30 seconds, until coarsely chopped.

4   Transfer the chopped hazelnuts to a large heatproof bowl and add the chocolate, butter, and ¾ cup (170 milliliters) of the cream. Set the bowl over a bain-marie (see page 30) and heat until the chocolate and butter have melted. Remove the bowl from the heat.

5   In a separate heatproof bowl, combine the egg yolks and sugar. Place the bowl over the same bain-marie and cook, whisking continuously, for about 4 minutes, until the egg yolks thicken enough to leave a ribbon on the surface when the whisk is lifted out. Remove from the heat.

6   While whisking, add the egg yolks to the chocolate mixture, then the salt.

RECIPE CONTINUES

7   Using a stand mixer fitted with the whisk attachment or a handheld electric mixer, whip the remaining 1 cup (225 milliliters) cream until soft peaks form. Fold the whipped cream into the chocolate mixture.

8   Line a 9 x 5 inch loaf pan with two layers of plastic wrap. Pour the chocolate mixture into the prepared pan. Gently tap the pan on your countertop to remove any air bubbles.

9   Refrigerate until set, 5 to 6 hours. Once set, use the plastic wrap to lift the pâté out of the pan. Turn out onto a serving platter or other flat surface to cut. Using a warm, wet knife, cut slices about ½ inch thick.

10 Serve cold, topped with whipped cream. Store leftovers in the refrigerator, covered, for up to 7 days.

SILKY-SMOOTH CHOCOLATE SOUP

MAKES 6 SERVINGS

3 cups (675 milliliters) full fat milk

1 cup (225 milliliters) heavy cream

2 cups (12 ounces/ 340 grams) chopped bittersweet chocolate

3 tablespoons cornstarch

2 tablespoons water

½ teaspoon salt

2 teaspoons pure vanilla extract

Whipped cream, for serving

Grated chocolate, for serving (optional)

Why eat an ordinary bar of chocolate when you can enjoy a sophisticated and highly indulgent chocolate soup? Incredibly decadent but not overly sweet, this rich and creamy dessert gets its sweetness from bittersweet chocolate, melted and whisked into milk and cream and finished off with a little salt and vanilla. Serving this warm is a must, as is topping it with dollops of freshly whipped cream. Grate some chocolate over the top to really gild the lily. You can also make this in a very short amount of time, which will impress all your guests. Soup for dessert is starting to sound pretty good, isn't it?

1 In a medium saucepan, combine the milk and cream and bring to a simmer over medium heat.

2 Reduce the heat to low, add the chocolate, and whisk until the chocolate starts to melt.

3 Meanwhile, in a small bowl, mix the cornstarch and water together to form a runny paste. This will be stiff at first, but keep mixing until combined and smooth.

4 When the chocolate mixture comes to a simmer, add the cornstarch paste and cook, whisking continuously, for 1 minute, until the soup is thick and smooth.

5 Reduce the heat to very low heat and simmer for 2 to 3 minutes to cook out the raw taste of the cornstarch.

6 Turn off the heat and whisk in the salt and vanilla. Pass the soup through a sieve for a smooth, silky result.

7 Divide the soup among six serving bowls and garnish with some freshly whipped cream and grated chocolate, if you'd like. Enjoy warm.

CREAMY RICE PUDDING

½ cup (115 grams) Arborio rice

4⅔ cups (1.2 liters) whole milk

6 tablespoons (85 grams) sugar

2 tablespoons (28 grams) butter

⅛ teaspoon ground nutmeg (see Note)

Raspberry jam, for serving

NOTE

I strongly urge you not to leave out the nutmeg—it brings the whole dish to life.

One dessert that made regular appearances on our dinner table when I was young was rice pudding, usually on winter evenings after we came in out of the cold. My mum would make it with plump "pudding rice," which is much like Arborio, the rice I use in my recipe here, and she'd serve it in individual bowls with a little jam on the side. We would dig into it while it was still warm, making sure to get a little jam mixed in with the pudding in every spoonful. This one's easy enough to make for a midweek after-dinner treat. Go ahead and give it a go.

1   In a medium saucepan, combine the rice, milk, sugar, butter, and nutmeg. Cover and bring to a simmer over medium heat.

2   Reduce the heat to low and let the rice gently bubble away, stirring occasionally to keep the rice from sticking to the pan, for 35 to 40 minutes, until the rice is fully cooked and has absorbed most of the liquid, leaving a creamy sauce.

3   Serve the rice pudding hot in bowls with some jam on top. Store any leftovers in the fridge, covered, for up to 3 days.

DAD'S FAVORITE FOUR-INGREDIENT CRÈME BRÛLÉE

**2 cups (450 milliliters)
heavy cream**

**1 vanilla bean, halved
lengthwise**

6 large egg yolks

**¼ cup (57 grams) sugar,
plus about 6 tablespoons
for brûléeing**

NOTE

If you do not have
a kitchen torch, set
the ramekins on a
baking sheet and
slide them under
the broiler. Broil
until the sugar has
caramelized on
top. Just be careful
that your brûlées
don't get too warm
under the flame, or
the custards will
become very soft.

My dad is a huge food lover, and when my mum sets
something he likes in front of him, he claps his hands
together and says, "Oh baby—oh yeah!" Make him
something good, and he will love you forever. Crème brûlée
is his absolute favorite dessert and I love watching him crack
the caramel with the back of his spoon, a huge childlike smile
on his face. I have made a lot of crème brûlée at almost
every job I've ever had, but nothing compares to the taste
and texture of my mum's recipe right here.

1   Preheat the oven to 300°F (150°C). Set a large deep
    baking dish aside and bring a kettle of water to a boil.

2   Pour the cream into a medium saucepan, scrape the vanilla
    seeds into the cream, and add the pod. Bring the cream to
    a simmer over low heat.

3   Remove from the heat and let the flavors infuse for
    20 minutes.

4   In a medium bowl, whisk together the egg yolks and sugar.
    While whisking, slowly pour in the warm cream.

5   Pass your custard through a sieve to remove any lumps.
    Rinse off the vanilla pod and save it for another use.

6   Divide the custard among six 4-ounce ramekins. Place
    the ramekins in the large, deep baking dish. Carefully
    pour in enough boiling water to come halfway up the sides
    of the ramekins. (Take care not to get any water in the
    ramekins.) Carefully transfer the baking dish to the oven.

RECIPE CONTINUES

7 Bake for 25 to 30 minutes, until the custards are set around the edge but still have a slight jiggle in the middle. Carefully remove the baking dish from the oven and remove the ramekins from the water; let the custards cool completely.

8 Cover and refrigerate the custards for at least 4 hours. They will firm up once cold.

9 When ready to serve, sprinkle about 1 tablespoon sugar evenly over the top of each custard. With a kitchen torch, caramelize the sugar on top until it reaches a deep golden brown color.

10 Enjoy the crème brûlée just as it is. If you have any left over, store in the fridge, covered, for up to 3 days.

SALTED BUTTERSCOTCH POTS DE CRÈME

MAKES 10 POTS

4 tablespoons (½ stick/ 57 grams) butter

1 cup (170 grams) dark brown sugar

3 cups (675 milliliters) heavy cream

1 cup (225 milliliters) whole milk

1½ teaspoons pure vanilla extract

½ teaspoon salt

6 large egg yolks

Whipped cream, for serving

When I first met my husband, Kevin, we enjoyed some wonderful butterscotch pots de crème—a flavor we both love—at one of our favorite San Francisco restaurants. For our first anniversary, I made Kevin a homemade cookbook that included this recipe.

1   In a medium saucepan, heat the butter and brown sugar over medium heat, without stirring, until melted. Let the mixture simmer for 8 to 10 minutes, until a deep brown caramel forms. (You want to get the deep brown color, but take care not to let the caramel smoke or burn.)

2   Reduce the heat to low and slowly whisk in the cream and milk. The caramel will splatter and seize up, but keep on whisking and it will dissolve. Remove from the heat and stir in the vanilla and salt. Set aside to cool slightly.

3   In a medium bowl, whisk the egg yolks. Temper the egg yolks by adding a small amount of the warm butterscotch mixture to the egg yolks while constantly whisking. Once the yolks feel warm to the touch, pour the entire yolk mixture into the pot of caramel and whisk to combine.

4   Strain the custard through a sieve to remove any lumps. Divide it among ten small ramekins or mini mason jars. (You can make the custard up to 48 hours in advance and keep it in the fridge, covered, until you're ready to bake.)

5   Preheat the oven to 325°F (165°C). Set a large, deep baking dish aside and bring a kettle of water to a boil.

RECIPE CONTINUES

6   Place the ramekins in the large baking dish. Carefully pour in enough boiling water to come halfway up the sides of the ramekins. (Take care not to get any water in the ramekins.)

7   Bake for 25 to 30 minutes, until the custards are set around the edge but still have a jiggle in the middle; start checking for doneness around 25 minutes by tapping the side of each ramekin. Be careful not to overbake or they will become grainy.

8   Carefully remove the baking dish from the oven. Transfer the ramekins to a wire rack to cool to room temperature. Cover and refrigerate for at least 4 hours before serving, or store in the fridge, covered, for up to 3 days. Serve with a dollop of whipped cream on top.

VANILLA PANNA COTTA WITH ROASTED STRAWBERRIES

MAKES 6 SERVINGS

FOR THE PANNA COTTA

Vegetable oil, for the ramekins

¼ cup (58 milliliters) water

1 tablespoon powdered gelatin

2½ cups (565 milliliters) heavy cream

1 cup (225 milliliters) whole milk

½ cup (115 grams) sugar

2 teaspoons pure vanilla extract

FOR THE ROASTED STRAWBERRIES

3 cups (426 grams) strawberries

⅓ cup (71 grams) sugar

1 vanilla bean, split lengthwise

I love to blur the lines that define what to eat in the morning. If you think about it, the ingredients here are all commonly used at breakfast: milk, sugar, strawberries.

1   *To make the panna cotta:* Lightly brush six 6-ounce ramekins with vegetable oil and place them on a rimmed baking sheet (this makes them easy to transfer to the fridge).

2   Pour the water into a medium bowl and sprinkle the gelatin over the top. Whisk with a fork until smooth. Set aside for 5 minutes to allow the gelatin to soften (or "bloom"). It will look spongy when it's ready.

3   In a medium saucepan, combine the cream, milk, and sugar and bring to a simmer over medium heat. Simmer, stirring frequently, until the sugar has dissolved and the mixture is just starting to steam. Do not let it come to a boil. Remove from the heat.

4   While whisking, slowly pour the hot cream mixture over the gelatin and whisk to dissolve the gelatin. Stir in the vanilla.

5   Pass the custard through a fine-mesh sieve into a bowl to remove any bits of undissolved gelatin.

6   Divide the custard among the prepared ramekins and let cool completely. Cover with plastic wrap and refrigerate for at least 8 hours, or preferably overnight. Keep refrigerated for up to 3 days.

RECIPE CONTINUES

To help release the panna cottas, dip the bottoms of the ramekins in a little hot water.

7   *To make the roasted strawberries:* Preheat the oven to 400°C (200°F) and line a rimmed baking sheet with aluminum foil. Cut the strawberries in half and toss with the sugar in a bowl.

8   Scrape the vanilla seeds into the bowl with the strawberries. Add the pod and stir.

9   Spread the strawberries on the prepared baking sheet. Roast for 15 to 20 minutes, until the strawberries have softened and the juices in the pan are thick. Set aside to cool. (The roasted strawberries can be served warm or cold; refrigerate them in an airtight container for up to 5 days.)

10 To serve, turn your chilled panna cottas out of the ramekins onto individual serving plates. Spoon over some of the roasted strawberries and their juices.

COCONUT SEMIFREDDO WITH TROPICAL FRUIT SALSA

FOR THE COCONUT
SEMIFREDDO

**1 (14-ounce/
396-gram) can
sweetened condensed
milk (see page 311)**

**1 (13.5-ounce/
400-milliliter) can
unsweetened coconut
milk**

**1½ cups (340 milliliters)
heavy cream**

FOR THE TROPICAL
FRUIT SALSA

½ ripe mango, diced

10 strawberries, diced

**Grated zest and juice of
1 lime**

Dessert doesn't get much easier than this. This is a fun, tropical variation of my Three-Ingredient No-Churn Vanilla Ice Cream (page 236). Here I combine coconut milk with the condensed milk, fold in whipped cream, and freeze. All you need to do is cut it into slices and top it with a brightly colored, tangy mango-lime salsa (which is just as simple to make). It's pure elegance and creamy deliciousness.

1   *To make the semifreddo:* Line a 9 x 5-inch loaf pan with parchment paper, leaving a few inches overhanging on all sides (to help you remove the semifreddo from the pan once it's frozen).

2   In a medium saucepan, combine the condensed milk and coconut milk and bring to a simmer over high heat. Reduce the heat to maintain a simmer and cook for about 10 minutes, until thickened. Remove from the heat and set aside to cool completely.

3   Using a stand mixer fitted with the whisk attachment or a handheld electric mixer, beat the cream on high speed until stiff peaks form, 2 to 3 minutes.

4   Gently fold the cooled coconut milk mixture into the whipped cream. Pour the mixture into the prepared loaf pan. Cover and freeze for about 6 hours, until firm.

RECIPE CONTINUES

5   *To make the salsa:* In a small bowl, stir together the mango, strawberries, lime zest, and lime juice. Cover and refrigerate for at least 1 hour for the flavors to develop.

6   Before serving, let the semifreddo sit at room temperature for 10 minutes. Use the overhanging parchment to lift it out of the pan and set it on a serving platter (discard the parchment).

7   Serve nice, thick slices of the semifreddo with the salsa. Store any leftover semifreddo in the freezer, covered, for up to 6 weeks.

CHOCOLATE FLORENTINES

2 tablespoons
(28 grams) butter

½ cup (85 grams) light
brown sugar

¼ cup (71 grams) honey

2 tablespoons whole
milk

1 teaspoon pure vanilla
extract

⅓ cup (43 grams)
all-purpose flour

½ cup (71 grams)
almonds, finely chopped

1 cup (6 ounces/
170 grams) chopped
semisweet chocolate

NOTE

If you find the
florentines aren't as
crisp as you'd like
once they've cooled
completely (before
spreading them
with chocolate), you
can put them back
in the oven to bake
a little longer, about
5 minutes.

Florentines are pretty little lacy cookies, studded with sliced almonds and dipped in chocolate. These were in my childhood cookbook and I could not make enough of them. They are so simple to make and yet so elegant. Give these to close friends and loved ones.

1   Preheat the oven to 350°F (180°C). Line two cookie sheets with parchment paper.

2   In a small saucepan, combine the butter, brown sugar, honey, milk, and vanilla and bring to a simmer over medium heat. Cook gently, without stirring, for 2 to 3 minutes, until the mixture becomes a golden caramel. Remove from the heat.

3   Whisk in the flour and almonds. Set the dough aside to cool for 20 minutes, until scoopable.

4   Using a teaspoon, scoop out balls of dough, gently round them in your hand, and place them on the prepared cookie sheets (9 balls on each cookie sheet). Leave some space between them, as they'll spread a lot during baking.

5   Bake for 18 to 20 minutes, until the cookies are a rich golden brown. Let cool on the cookie sheets for 15 minutes before transferring to a wire rack to cool completely. The cookies will harden as they cool.

6   Melt the chocolate in a small heatproof bowl in the microwave or over a bain-marie (see page 30).

7   Spread a little melted chocolate over the bottom of each cookie and return to the rack, chocolate side up. Let the chocolate set for about 30 minutes, until hardened.

8   Store in an airtight container at room temperature for up to 3 days.

BAKED CINNAMON-SUGAR CHURROS

MAKES 25 TO 30
CHURROS

**FOR THE
CHURRO DOUGH**

**1 cup (225 milliliters)
water**

**½ cup (1 stick/
115 grams) butter**

**2 tablespoons light
brown sugar**

¼ teaspoon salt

**1 cup (142 grams)
all-purpose flour**

**3 large eggs, at room
temperature**

**½ teaspoon pure vanilla
extract**

**FOR THE
CINNAMON-SUGAR**

½ cup (115 grams) sugar

**1 teaspoon ground
cinnamon**

¼ teaspoon salt

**Melted butter, for
brushing the churros**

**1 recipe Rich Chocolate
Ganache (page 284), for
serving**

Churros are one of my most popular recipes. Maybe it's because mine are baked instead of deep-fried, so they aren't quite as guilt-inducing as the traditional version. Or perhaps it's because while I was creating my version, I once mistakenly put salt in the cinnamon-sugar and ended up with a salty-sweet coating—a delicious happy accident that I repeat every time I make these now. Either way, be sure to serve these with little dishes of luscious, rich chocolate ganache—perfect for dipping.

1   Preheat the oven to 400°F (200°C). Line two cookie sheets with parchment paper.

2   *To make the churro dough:* In a medium saucepan, combine the water, butter, brown sugar, and salt and bring to a simmer over medium heat. As soon as the butter has melted and the mixture is simmering, whisk in the flour. Whisk until there are no lumps and a ball of dough has formed.

3   Reduce the heat to low and cook the dough, stirring continuously with a wooden spoon, for about 1 minute. The dough will clump and pull away from the sides of the pan. Take it off the heat and set aside.

4   In a measuring cup, whisk together the eggs and vanilla. Add a little bit of the egg mixture to the dough, stirring and mashing with a wooden spoon to break up the dough until loosened, then stir well until the egg mixture has been incorporated and the mixture has the appearance of mashed potatoes. Continue adding the remaining egg

RECIPE CONTINUES

mixture, a little at a time, until combined and you have a smooth dough.

5 Transfer the dough to a piping bag fitted with a large star tip.

6 Pipe the dough into 4-inch-long churros on the prepared cookie sheets, leaving about 2 inches between them. Make sure to pipe them nice and thick by applying even pressure on the bag and piping slowly.

7 Sprinkle some water over the cookie sheets (this will create steam in the oven, which will help the churros rise).

8 Bake for 18 to 22 minutes, until golden brown. Turn off the oven and leave the churros inside for 10 minutes to dry them a little (this step helps them keep their shape and not go flat once they cool).

9 *Meanwhile, to make the cinnamon-sugar:* Combine the sugar, cinnamon, and salt in a large zip-top bag, seal, and shake until mixed well.

10 While the churros are still warm, take them straight from the oven and brush them all over with a little melted butter. Toss them in the bag of cinnamon-sugar until well coated. (It is best to do this when the churros are warm and fresh from the oven, as the sugar will stick better.)

11 Enjoy your churros warm, with the chocolate ganache on the side for dipping. Store any leftover churros in an airtight container at room temperature for up to 24 hours.

DINNER PARTY
CHOCOLATE PROFITEROLES

**MAKES 30
PROFITEROLES**

½ cup (115 milliliters)
water

4 tablespoons (½ stick/
57 grams) butter

½ teaspoon salt

1 cup (142 grams)
all-purpose flour

2 large eggs, at room
temperature

Whipped cream,
for filling

1 recipe Rich Chocolate
Ganache (page 284), for
drizzling

My mum had two or three trusted recipes that she always turned to when making dessert for guests, and these profiteroles (or cream puffs) were one of them. She would serve them dripping with chocolate sauce, and if we were very lucky, there would be some left over and in the morning we would eat them straight out of the fridge. Profiteroles were also a specialty of my brother, George, and he would make them specifically so he could bring them to school to share with his friends in the dorms. I like to fill the profiteroles with whipped cream and cover them with chocolate ganache, just like my mum did.

1   Preheat the oven to 425°F (220°C). Line two cookie sheets with parchment paper.

2   In a medium saucepan, combine the water, butter, and salt and bring to a boil over medium heat.

3   Add the flour all at once and whisk vigorously to get out any lumps. Cook, stirring continuously with a wooden spoon, for about 1 minute, until the dough pulls away from the side of the pan and forms a ball around your spoon. Remove from the heat.

4   Whisk the eggs in a small bowl. Add a little bit of the eggs to the dough and, using a wooden spoon, quickly stir until the egg is combined (it will start out looking like a mess, but just keep stirring and it will come together). Add the remaining egg, a little at a time, until it's all combined and the dough is smooth and shiny.

RECIPE CONTINUES

5   Transfer the dough to a piping bag fitted with a large round tip.

6   Pipe the dough onto the prepared cookie sheets in 1½-inch rounds, leaving about 2 inches between them. Wet your finger and smooth out any peaks on the tops of the rounds, so the peaks don't burn while baking.

7   Sprinkle some water over the cookie sheets (this will create steam in the oven, which will help the profiteroles rise).

8   Bake, without opening the oven door, for 12 to 15 minutes, until the profiteroles are golden brown all over and hollow-sounding when tapped. Transfer to a wire rack and let cool completely. (If not serving immediately, store the unfilled profiteroles for 24 hours in an airtight container at room temperature.)

9   Put the whipped cream in a piping bag fitted with a large round tip. Push the tip into the bottom of a profiterole and fill it with whipped cream. Repeat to fill the remaining profiteroles.

10 Drizzle the profiteroles with the chocolate ganache. Serve immediately, or store in an airtight container in the refrigerator for up to 6 hours before serving.

ROSY POACHED PEACHES WITH VANILLA

MAKES 6 SERVINGS

4 cups (900 milliliters) water

½ cup (115 grams) sugar

1 tablespoon fresh lemon juice

1 tablespoon rose water

1 vanilla bean, split lengthwise

6 firm peaches

Mascarpone cheese, for serving

This is a wonderful way to turn peaches that are on the firm side into something elegant enough to serve at a dinner party. Simmered in rose water and vanilla syrup, the peaches absorb a heady, floral Middle Eastern flavor, which is enhanced by the vanilla. You can find rose water at gourmet groceries or Middle Eastern markets. A dollop of mascarpone cheese, a richer, creamier variation of cream cheese, has a tangy taste that is a wonderful complement to the sweetness of the peaches. Crème fraîche also makes a nice accompaniment.

1 In a medium saucepan, combine the water, sugar, lemon juice, and rose water. Scrape the vanilla seeds into the sugar mixture and add the pod. Cook over medium heat, stirring, until the sugar has dissolved.

2 Add the peaches and bring to mixture to a simmer. Poach, turning occasionally, for 12 to 15 minutes, until the peaches are tender.

3 Remove from the heat and carefully lift out the peaches to cool on a platter; reserve the poaching syrup. (If not serving immediately, store the peaches in the fridge, immersed in the poaching syrup, for up to 4 days.)

4 Serve the peaches warm or cold, with mascarpone and some of the poaching syrup drizzled on top.

BOURBON BANANAS FOSTER

MAKES 4 SERVINGS

6 tablespoons (¾ stick/85 grams) butter

½ cup (85 grams) light brown sugar

¼ teaspoon ground cinnamon

4 ripe bananas, peeled and cut in half lengthwise

⅓ cup (71 milliliters) bourbon

Vanilla ice cream, for serving

If you need an impromptu last-minute dessert, try this classic: bananas sautéed in butter and brown sugar until caramelized, served warm with the sauce spooned over the top. A scoop of vanilla ice cream is a must and gets all yummy and melty from the heat of the bananas. Caramel and bananas are close friends when it comes to natural flavor combinations. When I'm feeling bold, I might add a little bourbon, which takes this dessert to a more adult place. The booze is optional, though, and the dish will taste very good without it, if it's not your thing.

1   In a large skillet, combine the butter, brown sugar, and cinnamon. Cook over medium heat, stirring, until the sugar has dissolved and the butter has melted.

2   Place the bananas in the pan, cut-side down, and cook for 2 to 3 minutes, until they just start to soften.

3   Gently turn the bananas over and cook for 2 to 3 minutes on the other side, until the bananas are soft and have begun to brown.

4   Remove the pan from the heat and carefully add the bourbon, standing back. Swirl the pan to incorporate the bourbon, then, using a long-necked lighter, carefully ignite the bourbon. When the flames subside, swirl the pan again to mix the sauce.

5   Serve the bananas immediately, with the bourbon sauce poured over the top and the ice cream.

Chapter 3

ROLLING PIN

ONCE I GOT THE HANG OF GETTING INTO THE KITCHEN and baking, I never shied away from more complicated recipes. I remember making sausage rolls—sausages encased in puff pastry—for the first time when I was about eleven years old, a big job for a young girl, one that requires enough patience and diligence to follow all the steps of making the puff pastry. The sausage rolls were terrific, which gave me the confidence to try all sorts of treats. At Christmastime, I would make little mince pies with citrus peel and maraschino cherries and sell them to my aunties. I still have the little cutters I used to make mistletoe decorations for the tops. I'm sure it cost my mum a fortune—I used all her best butter and handmade mincemeat—but I made myself some nice pocket money over the holidays. In this chapter, a rolling pin is the key piece of equipment you'll need to master things like my hugely popular Overnight Cinnamon Rolls (page 155) and gorgeous Rustic Raspberry & Lemon Tart (page 147).

PISTACHIO-ORANGE PALMIERS

MAKES 20 PALMIERS

¾ cup (115 grams) pistachios, coarsely chopped

3 tablespoons (36 grams) plus ¼ cup (43 grams) light brown sugar

Grated zest of 1 orange

1 recipe Foolproof Puff Pastry (page 299), or 1 sheet store-bought puff pastry

Whenever I went to our local bakery in Ireland, I was always tempted by the palmiers, which looked so pretty with their elegant shapes and delicate, crispy pastry. They are sometimes called other names, such as elephant ears, pig's ears, butterflies, French hearts, or palm trees. Whatever you want to call them, you will be amazed at how easy they are to make at home. Start with puff pastry, which is a simple matter to roll out. Then you sprinkle it with nuts, orange zest, and brown sugar, roll up the dough, and cut it into thin slices. Bake the slices, and you're done. The addition of pistachios makes these a little bit different from traditional recipes and gives them an appealing pop of green. Believe me, once you try this recipe, you'll forget all about the bakery version.

1   In a small bowl, stir together the pistachios, 3 tablespoons of the brown sugar, and the orange zest.

2   On a floured surface, roll out the puff pastry to about ¼ inch thick. With a knife, cut the pastry into a rectangle measuring 14 x 10 inches.

3   Sprinkle the pistachio mixture over the pastry and press it down gently with your hand.

4   Starting from one long side, roll up the pastry around the filling until you reach the center; repeat on the other side so both sides meet in the middle. Press together in the center so it holds its shape.

5   Rub the remaining ¼ cup (43 grams) brown sugar all over the outside of the pastry (this will create a crisp, crunchy cookie once baked). Wrap the dough in plastic wrap, place on a cookie sheet, and refrigerate for at least 30 minutes.

6   While the dough is chilling, preheat the oven to 375°F
     (190°C) and line two cookie sheets with parchment paper.

7   With a sharp knife, cut the pastry crosswise into ½-inch-
     thick pieces and put them on the prepared cookie sheets,
     leaving a little space between them, as they'll spread a bit.

8   Bake for 15 to 18 minutes, until golden brown. While
     warm, transfer to a wire rack to cool completely.

9   Store in an airtight container at room temperature for up
     to 2 days.

BLUEBERRY & ALMOND GALETTE

**2 cups (284 grams)
blueberries**

2 tablespoons sugar

2 tablespoons cornstarch

**1 teaspoon pure vanilla
extract**

**1 recipe Never-Fail Pie
Crust (page 296)**

**1 recipe Frangipane
(page 295)**

**1 large egg, beaten, for
egg wash**

**Vanilla ice cream,
for serving**

A galette is basically a pie that is formed by hand instead of being baked in a pie pan. This one is loaded with blueberries and frangipane, then the edge of the dough folded over just enough to enclose the filling, so that the beautiful fruit shows through in the center. This gives it a casual, rustic look that keeps it from feeling too fancy. Galettes make a great dessert for a barbecue or picnic.

1 Preheat the oven to 400°F (200°C). Line a rimmed baking sheet with parchment paper.

2 In a medium bowl, combine the blueberries, sugar, cornstarch, and vanilla. Set aside.

3 On a lightly floured work surface, roll out the pie dough to a 12-inch circle. Place the dough on the prepared baking sheet. Spoon the frangipane in the center of the dough, leaving a 3-inch border, then carefully pile on the blueberry mixture. Fold the edge of the dough up over the filling, leaving some blueberries exposed in the center. This is a rustic tart, so don't worry about making it perfect—it will bake up beautifully. Brush the dough with the egg to give the pastry a lovely shine.

4 Bake for 30 to 35 minutes, until the crust is golden brown.

5 Serve warm, with vanilla ice cream. Store any leftovers in the fridge, covered, for up to 3 days.

RHUBARB & ORANGE CUSTARD TARTS

1 pound (4 cups/
450 grams) chopped
rhubarb

⅓ cup (71 grams) sugar

¼ cup (60 milliliters)
water

1 tablespoon grated
orange zest

Butter, for the tart pans

1 recipe Never-Fail Pie
Crust (page 296)

1 recipe Simple Pastry
Cream (page 291)

When I was growing up, rhubarb was a pretty common ingredient in our desserts. As I started baking with it on my own, I always tried to give it a big and bold twist. Here the sweetness of orange curbs the tartness of the rhubarb, making them great flavor friends. These individual tarts are a relatively light end to a wonderful meal. Alternatively, you can make a single large pie; just fit the dough into a 9-inch pie pan.

1 In a medium saucepan, combine the rhubarb, sugar, water, and orange zest and bring to a simmer over medium-low heat. Simmer gently for 5 to 7 minutes, until the rhubarb is tender. Set aside to cool.

2 Generously butter nine 4-inch individual tart pans. On a lightly floured work surface, roll out the pie dough to a little thinner than ¼ inch thick. Using a 4½-inch round cookie cutter, cut out 9 circles. Place them in your tart tins and press the dough into the edges. With a fork, prick the dough all over to stop it from puffing up during baking. Put the tart shells on a baking sheet and chill for at least 1 hour.

3 When ready to bake, preheat the oven to 425°F (220°C).

4 Line each tart shell with parchment paper and fill with dried beans or other weights.

5 Bake the tart shells for 15 minutes. Remove the beans and parchment and bake for 4 to 5 minutes more, until the pastry is golden brown. Set aside to cool completely.

6 Fill each cooled tart shell with pastry cream almost to the top, then spoon 2 tablespoons of the rhubarb over each tart.

7 Store any leftovers in the fridge, covered, for up to 2 days.

MY ENGLISH BAKEWELL TART

MAKES 8 SERVINGS

1 recipe Never-Fail Pie Crust (page 296), chilled

½ cup (142 grams) raspberry jam

1 recipe Frangipane (page 295)

2 tablespoons slivered almonds

Whipped cream, for serving

A traditional English dessert, the Bakewell Tart is built in layers with an enticing mix of jam, frangipane (this is a bit like almond paste), and sliced almonds, all stacked in a crisp pie crust. My mum made this a lot when I was young, mostly for Sunday dessert, though as you can imagine, with seven of us in the family it didn't go very far!

1   Preheat the oven to 350°F (180°C). Grease a 9-inch pie pan.

2   Roll out the pie dough into a 13-inch round and lay it in the prepared pan. Trim away any excess dough from around the edge.

3   Spread the jam over the dough.

4   Carefully pour the frangipane mixture over the jam and then sprinkle the almonds on top.

5   Bake for 35 to 45 minutes, until golden brown. If the almonds begin to brown too quickly, cover the tart loosely with aluminum foil. Once baked, transfer to a wire rack to cool slightly.

6   Slice while still warm and serve with some whipped cream. Store any leftovers at room temperature, covered, for up to 4 days.

TOASTED PECAN PIE

MAKES 8 SERVINGS

1 recipe Never-Fail Pie Crust (page 296), chilled

6 large egg yolks

½ cup (142 grams) maple syrup

⅔ cup (115 grams) dark brown sugar

6 tablespoons (¾ stick/ 85 grams) butter, melted

¼ cup (57 milliliters) heavy cream

3 cups (425 grams) pecans, toasted (see page 161)

Vanilla ice cream, for serving

Pecan pie is not very common in Ireland, but after I found a recipe for it in an Australian cookbook I had lying around, I got curious and made it. I immediately loved it, but of course I had to put my own spin on it. Most pecan pie recipes use corn syrup, but I chose to use maple syrup instead so the filling had a lovely custardy texture and an extra layer of distinctive flavor. The pie was also really easy to make, so I found myself serving it frequently for Sunday lunch while I was working at a spa in Wexford, where it was a big hit.

1 Preheat the oven to 350°F (180°C). Grease a 9-inch pie pan.

2 Roll out the pie dough into a 13-inch round and lay it in the prepared pan. Trim away any excess dough from around the edge.

3 In a large bowl, whisk together the egg yolks, maple syrup, brown sugar, butter, and cream.

4 Finely chop 2 cups (283 grams) of the toasted pecans and add them to the egg mixture.

5 Pour the pecan mixture into the crust. Arrange the remaining 1 cup (142 grams) pecans over the top of the pie to create a nice finish.

6 Bake for 30 to 35 minutes, until the pie is set around the edges but still a little wobbly in the middle.

7 Serve warm, with vanilla ice cream. Store any leftovers at room temperature, covered, for up to 4 days.

CHOCOLATE LAVA PIE

MAKES 8 SERVINGS

1 recipe Never-Fail Pie Crust (page 296)

6 tablespoons (¾ stick/ 85 grams) butter

½ cup (3 ounces/ 85 grams) chopped bittersweet chocolate

2 large eggs plus 2 large egg yolks

¼ cup (57 grams) sugar

¼ cup (35 grams) all-purpose flour

Vanilla ice cream, for serving

When I worked at a restaurant in Wexford, my home town in Ireland, this was their bestseller. After making literally hundreds of these luscious chocolate tarts, I figured out the perfect timing to ensure that each one came out with just the right gooey chocolate center. I've tweaked the recipe here to make one big pie so you don't need to fuss with individual dishes. Follow the instructions exactly to create the creamy lava in the middle and when you serve it at a dinner party you'll get plenty of *ooohs* and *ahhs*.

1   Preheat the oven to 350°F (180°C).

2   Roll out the pie dough into a 13-inch round and lay it in the pie pan. Trim away any excess dough from around the edge.

3   Put the butter and chocolate in a small heatproof bowl and melt them together in the microwave or over a bain-marie (see page 30). Set aside to cool while you beat the eggs.

4   Using a stand mixer fitted with the whisk attachment or a handheld electric mixer, beat the eggs, egg yolks, and sugar on high speed until the mixture is really fluffy and pale in color and forms a ribbon on the surface when the beater is lifted out. This takes around 4 minutes.

5   Decrease the mixer speed to low and drizzle in the cooled chocolate mixture. Turn off the machine and run a spatula around the bowl to make sure all the chocolate is mixed in.

6   Sift the flour over the chocolate mixture and gently fold it in until combined.

7   Pour the chocolate filling into your pie crust.

8   Bake for 20 to 22 minutes, until the edges are set but the center still jiggles slightly; take care not to overbake— you want a fudgy middle. Set aside on a wire rack to cool slightly.

9   Serve warm, with vanilla ice cream. Store any leftovers in the fridge, covered, for up to 3 days.

PEACH **SLAB PIE**

MAKES 8 SERVINGS

¾ cup (170 grams) sugar

2 tablespoons cornstarch

½ teaspoon ground cinnamon

½ teaspoon ground ginger

⅛ teaspoon salt

2 pounds peaches, pitted and sliced (6 cups/852 grams)

2 tablespoons fresh lemon juice

2 recipes Never-Fail Pie Crust (page 296)

1 large egg, beaten, for egg wash

Vanilla ice cream, for serving

Instead of using a traditional pie plate, a slab pie is made in a rectangular baking pan, making it great for a big crowd. This is a perfect recipe to reach for when you find lots of ripe peaches at the farmers' market or at your local grocery. Here I finish off the pie with a pretty lattice top crust. Serve it cut into squares at a summer picnic with all your friends and family.

1   Preheat the oven to 400°F (200°C). Grease a 9 x 13-inch rimmed baking sheet.

2   In a medium bowl, mix together the sugar, cornstarch, cinnamon, ginger, and salt. Add the peaches and lemon juice and toss to coat. Set aside.

3   Divide the pie dough into two pieces, roughly two-thirds and one-third. Roll out the larger piece of dough to a rectangle about 11 x 14 inches. Lay the dough into the prepared baking sheet, letting any excess hang over the edge.

4   Pour the peach filling into the crust and spread it evenly. Brush the rim of the dough with a little beaten egg.

5   Roll out the remaining piece of dough into a rectangle ⅛ inch thick. Cut it into strips and arrange them in a lattice design over the top of the pie, weaving the strips over and under. Trim away the overhanging dough. With your fingers, crimp the dough all the way around the edge to seal, then brush the dough all over with the beaten egg.

6   Bake for 35 to 40 minutes, until crust is golden brown and the filling is bubbling. Transfer to a wire rack to cool slightly before slicing.

7   Serve warm or at room temperature, with ice cream. Store leftovers in the refrigerator, covered, for up to 3 days.

CARAMELIZED BANANA TARTE TATIN

1 recipe Foolproof Puff Pastry (page 299), or 1 sheet store-bought puff pastry

6 tablespoons (85 grams) butter, softened

⅔ cup (115 grams) light brown sugar

4 or 5 medium bananas, peeled and sliced 1 inch thick

Vanilla ice cream, for serving

I love bananas so much that any recipe that showcases them is going to make me a happy woman. This one is a take on a traditional French tarte tatin, but instead of apples, I call for my beloved bananas. I use a recipe for puff pastry that I got from my mum, which takes a little less time to make than the classic version and still puffs up nicely.

1 Preheat the oven to 400°F (200°C).

2 On a floured surface, roll out the puff pastry to about ¼ inch thick. With a knife, cut out a 10-inch circle of pastry. Transfer the pastry to a cookie sheet, cover, and refrigerate until needed.

3 Place a 10-inch skillet over medium heat and add the butter and brown sugar. Cook, stirring until the sugar has melted. Place the bananas around the skillet, cut side down. Pack them in tight for the prettiest presentation. Let the bananas cook, undisturbed, for 1 to 2 minutes.

4 Top the bananas with the circle of puff pastry. With a knife, pierce some holes in the pastry to allow steam to escape.

5 Bake for 20 to 25 minutes, until the pastry is golden brown and the filling is bubbling. Transfer the skillet to a wire rack to cool for 5 minutes.

6 While the tarte tatin is still warm (don't let it cool too much, or the caramel with set and it will be difficult to turn out), carefully cover the top of the skillet with a serving platter. Holding them together, invert the pan and the platter to turn your tarte tatin out onto the platter.

7 Serve warm, with a big scoop of vanilla ice cream. Store leftovers in the fridge, covered, for up to 1 day.

RUSTIC RASPBERRY & LEMON TART

MAKES 6 TO 8 SERVINGS

1 recipe Foolproof Puff
Pastry (page 299),
or 1 sheet store-bought
puff pastry

1 large egg, beaten,
for egg wash

½ cup (115 grams)
mascarpone cheese

2 tablespoons granulated
sugar

1 recipe Easy Lemon
Curd (page 292)

4 cups (568 grams)
raspberries

Confectioners' sugar,
for serving

Nothing lifts my spirits like ripe, red raspberries, and this free-form tart shows them off in the manner they deserve. Rather than fitting the dough into a pan, I cut the pastry into a rectangle and create a border that will hold in the filling. The filling is a mixture of mascarpone and my Easy Lemon Curd, a combination that makes this taste a bit like cheesecake. Arrange the raspberries in a pretty pattern over the top and then dust it with confectioners' sugar right before serving. Other berries would work as well, including strawberries, blueberries, or blackberries (or a combination!).

1   Preheat the oven to 425°F (220°C). Line a rimmed baking sheet with parchment paper.

2   On a lightly floured work surface, roll out the puff pastry to about ⅛ inch thick. Cut it into a 10 x 12-inch rectangle.

3   Place the pastry on the prepared baking sheet. With a sharp knife, lightly cut a ½-inch border all the way around, without cutting all the way through the pastry. Imagine you are creating a frame around the pastry. Using a fork, prick the pastry all over inside the border to stop it from puffing up during baking. Brush the entire tart with the egg wash.

4   Bake for 12 to 15 minutes, until golden brown. If the center puffed up during baking, press it back down with your hand. Set aside to cool completely.

RECIPE CONTINUES

5   In a medium bowl, combine the mascarpone, granulated sugar, and lemon curd. Beat with a handheld electric mixer or by hand until smooth.

6   Carefully spread your lemon mixture over the center of the cooled tart crust. Arrange the raspberries neatly over the filling.

7   To serve, dust generously with confectioners' sugar and cut into slices. This is best eaten the same day, but leftovers can be stored in the refrigerator, covered, for up to 24 hours.

BUTTERY ALMOND BREAKFAST PASTRY

MAKES 8 SERVINGS

1 recipe Foolproof Puff Pastry (page 299), or 1 sheet store-bought puff pastry

2 cups (450 grams) Frangipane (page 295)

1 large egg, beaten, for egg wash

3 tablespoons sliced almonds

1 recipe Vanilla Glaze (page 283)

This sweet treat makes great use of my Foolproof Puff Pastry—here it's stuffed with creamy almond filling. I love the flavor of almonds, so I spread the puff pastry with frangipane (basically almond paste) and then sprinkle it with sliced almonds that become nicely toasted after baking. Both light and rich, this pastry makes a great addition to a breakfast or brunch menu.

1   Preheat the oven to 400°F (200°C). Line a cookie sheet with parchment paper.

2   Lightly flour your work surface and roll out the puff pastry to roughly ¼ inch thick. With a sharp knife, cut the pastry into a rectangle measuring about 10 x 14 inches, then slice it lengthwise down the middle to make two 5 x 14-inch rectangles.

3   Set one puff pastry rectangle on the prepared cookie sheet. Spread the frangipane lengthwise down the center, leaving a ¾-inch perimeter all the way around. (This may seem like a lot of filling, but it's the best part!)

4   Brush the perimeter with a little of the beaten egg (this will help seal the pastry). Lay the second piece of pastry on top and, with a fork, press the two pieces together all the way around to seal up the edges. With a knife, cut a

RECIPE CONTINUES

few vents in the top of the pastry to allow steam to escape as it bakes. Brush the pastry generously with the beaten egg and sprinkle the almonds on top.

5   Bake for 10 minutes, then lower the oven temperature to 375°F (190°C) and bake for 20 to 22 minutes more, until the puff pastry turns a rich golden brown. Transfer to a wire rack and let cool for 15 minutes.

6   While still warm, drizzle the pastry with the glaze and cut into slices. Store any leftovers in an airtight container at room temperature for up to 2 days.

HOMEMADE JELLY DOUGHNUTS

**MAKES 10 OR 11
DOUGHNUTS**

3¼ cups (454 grams)
all-purpose flour

1¼ cups (282 grams)
sugar

2¼ teaspoons instant
yeast

2 teaspoons salt

1 cup (225 milliliters)
whole milk

⅓ cup (71 milliliters)
water

2 tablespoons
(28 grams) butter

1 tablespoon pure vanilla
extract

3 cups (675 milliliters)
vegetable oil, for frying

¾ cup (213 grams)
strawberry jam

One of life's most sinful pleasures is definitely the jelly
doughnut, with its generous amount of strawberry jam inside
a lightly fried, airy dough. These doughnuts take a bit longer
to make than other desserts, but the payoff is well worth
the wait, I promise you. And you don't need to relegate
them to breakfast, either—they make an excellent end to
dinner as well.

1   In the bowl of a stand mixer fitted with the dough hook,
    combine the flour, ¼ cup (57 grams) of the sugar, the
    yeast, and the salt and mix briefly to combine.

2   In a large measuring cup or small saucepan, combine the
    milk, water, and butter. Heat in the microwave or on the
    stovetop over low heat until lukewarm and the butter has
    melted, about 1 minute. Stir in the vanilla.

3   With the mixer on low speed, slowly add the milk mixture
    (see Note) and mix for 2 minutes to wake up the yeast.
    Run a spatula under the dough to make sure everything is
    mixed well.

4   Increase the speed to medium and mix until the dough has
    come together and is smooth, 6 to 8 minutes.

5   Grease a large bowl with oil. Place the dough in the bowl
    and turn the dough to coat it lightly with oil. Cover the
    bowl with plastic wrap and let the dough rise at room
    temperature until doubled in size, 1½ to 2 hours.

6   Once it has risen, turn out the dough onto a floured work
    surface and roll it out to ¾ inch thick.

RECIPE CONTINUES

7   Using a round 3-inch cutter, cut out your doughnuts. (You can prepare the doughnuts to this stage up to 1 day in advance; cover them with plastic wrap and refrigerate. When you're ready to proceed, let them come to room temperature and rise a little, about 30 minutes.)

8   Cover the doughnuts with plastic wrap and let them rise at room temperature for 25 to 30 minutes.

9   Heat the oil in a large skillet over medium-low heat. Set a wire rack over a double layer of paper towels. Put the remaining 1 cup (225 grams) sugar in a shallow bowl.

10 To make sure your oil is the right temperature, put a scrap of dough in the oil: if it's hot enough, the dough should puff up and be golden brown after cooking for about 2 minutes per side. Working in batches, carefully place the doughnuts in the hot oil (be careful, as the oil will be very hot). Fry for about 3 minutes per side, until deep golden brown. Do not walk away from the pan at any stage of frying. Use a slotted spoon to remove each doughnut from the oil, letting any excess oil drip back into the pan. Toss in the sugar to coat while still warm, then transfer to the wire rack to cool for about 15 minutes before filling. Repeat to cook the remaining doughnuts.

11 When the doughnuts are cool to the touch, gently poke a wooden skewer lengthwise through the center of each doughnut, stopping around three-quarters of the way through. Swirl it around to create an opening for your filling.

12 Put the jam in a piping bag fitted with a small round piping tip. Insert the tip as far as you can into the hole in your doughnut. Gently squeeze in about 2 tablespoons of the jam, or enough jam that the doughnut plumps up. Set aside on a platter and repeat to fill the remaining doughnuts.

13 These are best enjoyed the same day they are made, but leftovers can be stored in an airtight container at room temperature for up to 24 hours.

OVERNIGHT CINNAMON ROLLS

MAKES 10 ROLLS

FOR THE CINNAMON ROLL DOUGH

3½ cups (497 grams) all-purpose flour

1 tablespoon instant yeast

2 teaspoons salt

1 cup (225 milliliters) whole milk

⅓ cup (71 milliliters) water

¼ cup (85 grams) honey

4 tablespoons (57 grams) butter

2 large eggs, at room temperature

FOR THE FILLING

½ cup (1 stick/ 115 grams) butter, melted

1¼ cups (213 grams) light brown sugar

2½ tablespoons ground cinnamon

1 cup (142 grams) chopped toasted pecans

1 recipe Cream Cheese Glaze (page 280)

You have got to make these cinnamon rolls! Just mix up the dough and leave it in the fridge to proof. The next morning, all you need to do is roll out the dough, fill it with a mixture of butter, brown sugar, cinnamon, and toasted pecans, and cut them into rolls. As they bake, your whole kitchen will be filled with their addictive aroma, drawing the attention of your entire household. Make these fresh cinnamon rolls for a bunch of hungry family members or friends, and they will love you forever.

1 *To make the dough:* In a very large bowl, combine the flour, yeast, and salt.

2 In a measuring cup, combine the milk, water, honey, and butter. Microwave the mixture for about 1 minute, until slightly warmed and the butter has melted.

3 Whisk the eggs into the milk mixture.

4 Stir the wet ingredients into the dry ingredients to make a sticky dough; there should be no lumps of flour left. Scrape down the dough from the sides of the bowl. The dough will appear soft; that is perfect. Cover the bowl and let the dough rise at room temperature for at least 2 hours, or until doubled in size.

5 Refrigerate the dough for at least 8 hours, or preferably overnight. (The dough can be refrigerated for up to 3 days before using.)

6 *Meanwhile, to make the filling:* Combine the melted butter, brown sugar, and cinnamon in a bowl and stir until smooth. Set aside to firm up.

RECIPE CONTINUES

7   When you are ready to make the cinnamon rolls, butter a deep 9 x 13-inch baking pan.

8   Transfer the dough to a floured work surface and roll it out into a rectangle roughly 25 x 11 inches. Spread the filling evenly over the dough, leaving a narrow margin around the edges. Scatter the pecans over the filling.

9   Starting from one long edge, gently roll the dough into a log. Slice the log into ten 3-inch-thick rolls and set them in the prepared baking pan in two rows of five rolls each. (At this point, you can cover the rolls and refrigerate them overnight to bake the following morning. Let them come to room temperature before baking.)

10 Cover the pan with plastic wrap and let the rolls rise at room temperature for 45 minutes to 1 hour, until they have puffed up and spread into each other.

11 Meanwhile, preheat the oven to 375°F (190°C).

12 Bake the rolls for 40 to 45 minutes, until they're a deep golden brown. Transfer the pan to a wire rack and let cool for 15 minutes.

13 While the rolls are still warm, spread the cream cheese glaze generously over the top and devour them immediately. Store any leftovers at room temperature, covered, for up to 24 hours.

Chapter 4

BAKING PANS

YOU ONLY NEED A FEW ESSENTIAL PANS TO MAKE ALL the recipes in this chapter. In my mum's kitchen in Ireland, there was one 8-inch square tin that we used for almost everything. I'll bet a lot of you have pans that were passed down to you from your mum or granny that you still use today. One reason I hang on to my square pan is because it's the perfect size for baking White Chocolate & Pecan Blondies (page 161). But the real reason I love that pan so much is that I have so many wonderful childhood memories of using it while baking with my family. As I've gotten older, I've expanded my collection of baking pans, and now I have a springform pan for making things like Baked Blueberry Cheesecake (page 178), and 6-inch cake pans, which make the most lovely three-layer cakes.

WHITE CHOCOLATE & PECAN BLONDIES

1 cup (2 sticks/ 225 grams) butter, melted

2 cups (340 grams) light brown sugar

1 tablespoon pure vanilla extract

2 large eggs, at room temperature

2 cups (284 grams) all-purpose flour

1 teaspoon salt

1½ cups (9 ounces/ 255 grams) white chocolate chips

1 cup (142 grams) pecans, toasted and chopped

NOTE

Toasting nuts before adding them to your baking makes the world of difference. Spread them over a rimmed baking sheet and toast them in the oven at 350°F (180°C) for 10 to 12 minutes, until lightly browned.

Brown sugar and butter are what make blondies so incredibly addictive. Most times, they are made with chocolate chips and sometimes butterscotch chips, but when I tried them with white chocolate and toasted pecans, a new blondie was born. Give them a go and you'll see what I mean.

1   Preheat the oven to 350°F (180°C). Grease an 8-inch square cake pan and line it with parchment paper.

2   In a medium bowl, stir together the melted butter, brown sugar, and vanilla.

3   Whisk in the eggs one at a time until well combined.

4   Using a large metal spoon, fold in the flour, salt, chocolate chips, and pecans. Pour the batter into the prepared pan.

5   Bake for about 30 minutes, until the top is golden brown and the middle is just set. Don't be tempted to bake them for longer than that, or you won't get gooey centers. Let the blondies cool completely in the pan.

6   Turn the blondies out onto a cutting board and cut into 9 squares. Enjoy warm, or cover and store at room temperature for up to 3 days.

THE FUDGIEST GIANT BROWNIES

MAKES 9 TO 12 BROWNIES

2½ cups (565 grams) sugar

½ cup (115 milliliters) water

⅔ cup (4 ounces/ 115 grams) coarsely chopped bittersweet chocolate

1½ cups (213 grams) all-purpose flour

⅔ cup (76 grams) unsweetened cocoa powder

½ teaspoon baking powder

1 teaspoon salt

4 large eggs, at room temperature

1 cup (225 milliliters) vegetable oil

2 teaspoons pure vanilla extract

1 cup (6 ounces/ 170 grams) chocolate chips, plus more for topping

Vanilla ice cream and hot fudge sauce, for serving (optional)

If you like your brownies really thick and fudgy all the way through like I do, you've come to the right place. Be careful when they go into the oven, though—you can't test for doneness like you do with other baked goods because they are so moist: A wooden toothpick stuck into the brownies will never come out clean. Be sure to take them out of the oven after 35 minutes, no longer, before they begin to dry out. I would make these for Sunday lunch when I was a junior chef at a spa in Wexford, Ireland—the boss didn't work on Sundays, so that was the time I could experiment. I would cut them in large squares, and they were so rich, the patrons sometimes had a hard time finishing them. Here they're cut into bigger squares, but you could cut them any size you like.

1 Preheat the oven to 350°F (180°C). Grease a 9 x 13-inch cake pan and line it with parchment paper.

2 In a small saucepan, combine the sugar, water, and chocolate and heat over medium heat, gently stirring, until the chocolate and sugar have melted. (This step can also be done in the microwave.) Set aside to cool.

3 Sift together the flour, cocoa powder, baking powder, and salt into a large bowl. Mix until combined.

4 Whisk the oil, eggs, and vanilla into the cooled chocolate mixture.

5 Add the chocolate mixture to the dry ingredients and mix until just combined. Fold in the chocolate chips. Do not over mix, as it will toughen the brownies.

6 Pour the batter into the prepared pan. Smooth the top with a spatula and top with additional chocolate chips.

NOTE

These brownies freeze really well. When you are faced with a dessert emergency, take one from the freezer and microwave it for about 1 minute.

7 Bake for 30 to 35 minutes. Take care not to overbake, or they won't be as fudgy on the inside. Let cool fully in the pan on a wire rack.

8 Turn the brownie block out onto a flat surface and cut it into 9 or 12 squares.

9 Serve warm, with vanilla ice cream and a drizzle of hot fudge sauce, if desired. Store in an airtight container at room temperature for up to 4 days.

GEMMA'S ULTIMATE BANANA BREAD

MAKES 1 LOAF

1½ cups (213 grams) all-purpose flour

¾ cup (64 grams) rolled oats (preferably quick-cooking)

⅔ cup (142 grams) sugar

2 teaspoons ground cinnamon

2 teaspoons baking powder

1 teaspoon salt

¼ teaspoon baking soda

3 medium bananas, mashed

2 large eggs

⅓ cup (71 milliliters) whole milk

¼ cup (57 milliliters) vegetable oil

1½ teaspoons pure vanilla extract

Everyone likes this banana bread! It's one of the most popular recipes I've ever created. It's on the unusual side because I've included oatmeal in the batter, which makes it incredibly moist and stick-to-your-ribs satisfying. It would make a very fine breakfast.

1 Preheat the oven to 350°F (180°C). Grease a 9 x 5-inch loaf pan and line it with parchment paper.

2 In a large bowl, stir together the flour, oats, sugar, cinnamon, baking powder, salt, and baking soda.

3 In a separate bowl, whisk together the bananas, eggs, milk, oil, and vanilla.

4 Pour the wet ingredients into the dry ingredients and mix until just combined. Do not overmix, as this can make the banana bread tough.

5 Pour the batter into the prepared pan.

6 Bake for about 55 minutes, until a toothpick inserted into the center of the bread comes out clean. Set the pan on a wire rack and let cool for 20 minutes, then turn the banana bread out onto the rack to cool completely.

7 Store at room temperature, wrapped in plastic wrap, for up to 3 days.

BEST-EVER CARROT CAKE

1¼ cups (170 grams) self-rising flour (see page 304)

½ teaspoon baking soda

1 teaspoon ground cinnamon

¾ cup (128 grams) light brown sugar

⅔ cup (150 milliliters) vegetable oil

2 large eggs, at room temperature

2 cups (225 grams) finely grated carrots (about 3 medium)

½ cup (71 grams) raisins

1 recipe Cream Cheese Glaze (page 280)

3 tablespoons chopped walnuts (optional)

My sister Julie makes the best carrot cake ever, and I had to share it with you. I make it in a loaf pan, drizzle it with a lot of Cream Cheese Glaze, and cut it into slices. When we were kids, our family kept carrot cake in an old biscuit tin with a lid, usually one that once held cookies we bought at Christmastime and which we saved for just this reason. We weren't the only family to do this and to this day, a biscuit tin filled with cake is commonly found in kitchens all over Ireland.

1   Preheat the oven to 350°F (180°C). Grease a 9 x 5-inch loaf pan and line it with parchment paper.

2   Sift together the flour, baking soda, cinnamon, and brown sugar into a medium bowl. Set aside.

3   Using a stand mixer fitted with the paddle attachment or a handheld electric mixer, beat the oil and eggs on high speed until really thick and pale in color.

4   Gently fold in the flour mixture with a large metal spoon until just combined. Fold in the carrots and raisins.

5   Pour the batter into the prepared pan. Bake for 50 to 55 minutes, until a toothpick inserted into the middle comes out clean. Set aside on a wire rack to cool completely.

6   Turn the cake out of the pan onto a cutting board and slice it in half horizontally. Spread a layer of the cream cheese glaze on the bottom half, then sandwich with the top layer. Drizzle the remaining glaze over the top of the loaf and sprinkle with walnuts, if using.

7   Cut big slices to serve. Store in an airtight container at room temperature for up to 3 days.

CINNAMON ROLL CAKE

MAKES 1 LOAF

2 cups (284 grams) all-purpose flour

1½ cups (340 grams) sugar

1 teaspoon baking powder

½ teaspoon salt

1¼ cups (284 milliliters) buttermilk

1 large egg

1 teaspoon pure vanilla extract

¼ cup (57 milliliters) vegetable oil

1 tablespoon ground cinnamon

1 recipe Cream Cheese Glaze (page 280)

Think of this as an American coffee cake with all the elements of a cinnamon roll—a cinnamon swirl on the inside and a drizzle of cream cheese glaze on the outside. If I gave this to my mum, she would say, "There's eating and drinking in this," her way of saying there is a lot going on in this cake.

1 Preheat the oven to 350°F (180°C). Grease a 9 x 5-inch loaf pan and line it with parchment paper.

2 In a large bowl, whisk together the flour, 1 cup (225 grams) of the sugar, the baking powder, and the salt.

3 In a large measuring cup, whisk together the buttermilk, egg, vanilla, and oil.

4 Add the wet ingredients to the dry ingredients and mix until just combined.

5 In a small bowl, combine the remaining ½ cup (115 grams) sugar and the cinnamon and mix well.

6 Spread half the batter in the prepared pan and sprinkle it with half the cinnamon-sugar. Pour the remaining batter into the pan and sprinkle the remaining cinnamon-sugar on top.

7 Using a knife, swirl the batter a few times to incorporate the cinnamon-sugar and create a swirl throughout the loaf.

8 Bake for 1 hour 20 minutes, or until a toothpick inserted into the center comes out clean. If the top is getting too brown, cover loosely with aluminum foil. Let the cake cool in the pan for 15 minutes, then turn it out onto a wire rack.

9 While the cake is still warm, spread it with the cream cheese glaze. Let cool completely.

10 Store airtight at room temperature for up to 4 days.

LEMON-BLUEBERRY LOAF

MAKES 1 LOAF

1½ cups (213 grams) all-purpose flour

½ teaspoon baking powder

¼ teaspoon baking soda

½ teaspoon salt

⅓ cup (71 grams) butter, softened

1 cup (225 grams) sugar

2 large eggs

1 teaspoon pure vanilla extract

1 tablespoon grated lemon zest

3 tablespoons fresh lemon juice

½ cup (115 grams) sour cream

1 cup (142 grams) blueberries

1 recipe Vanilla Glaze (page 283)

This is similar to a pound cake, but since pound cakes aren't common in Ireland, the proportions are a little different. You'll love its dense texture and buttery flavor, and the lemon-blueberry pairing is my favorite combination. Sour cream in the batter makes this very moist, and slices of the cake go particularly well at teatime when you have a few friends over for a chat.

1   Preheat the oven to 350°F (180°C). Grease a 9 x 5-inch loaf pan and line it with parchment paper.

2   In a large bowl, whisk together the flour, baking powder, baking soda, and salt.

3   Using a stand mixer fitted with the paddle attachment, or a handheld electric mixer, cream together the butter and sugar on high speed for 4 to 5 minutes, until soft and light in color.

4   Add the eggs, one at a time, and mix until well combined. Then mix in the vanilla, lemon zest, and lemon juice.

5   With the mixer on low speed, add the dry ingredients followed by the sour cream, alternating between the two. Fold in the blueberries. Run a spatula around the bowl to make sure everything is mixed well.

6   Pour the batter into the prepared pan and spread it evenly with a spatula.

7   Bake for 50 to 65 minutes, until a toothpick inserted into the center comes out clean. If the top is getting too brown, cover loosely with aluminum foil. Let the loaf cool in the pan for 20 minutes, then turn it out onto a wire rack to cool completely. Set the rack on a sheet of parchment paper.

8 While the cake is still warm, pour the vanilla glaze over the loaf. Let sit for 10 to 15 minutes so the glaze can set.

9 Store in an airtight container at room temperature for up to 4 days.

IRISH FAIRY CAKES

½ cup (1 stick/
115 grams) butter,
softened

½ cup (115 grams) sugar

2 large eggs, at room
temperature

¾ cup (115 grams)
self-rising flour
(see page 304)

2 tablespoons whole
milk

¼ cup (75 grams)
strawberry jam

1 recipe Vanilla
Buttercream Frosting
(page 276)

In Ireland, this is probably the first recipe almost every kid learns how to bake. My mum would let me make fairy cakes on my own, which kept me busy, though she wasn't always so happy with the trail of destruction I left in the kitchen. When she made them, my mum would put a little dollop of jam on top, though not all mums did. I've included it here, but it's optional, really.

1   Preheat the oven to 350°F (180°C). Line nine wells of a cupcake pan with paper liners.

2   Using a stand mixer fitted with the paddle attachment, or a handheld electric mixer, cream together the butter and sugar until fluffy and pale in color.

3   One by one, slowly incorporate the eggs and beat until well combined.

4   Add the flour and milk and carefully mix until you have a smooth batter.

5   Scoop the batter into the prepared cupcake pan, filling each well three-quarters of the way full.

6   Bake for 22 to 24 minutes, until the cupcakes are golden and spring back when pressed. Turn them out onto a wire rack and let cool completely.

7   Spoon 1 teaspoon of jam on top of each cupcake, then pipe or spread a swirl of buttercream frosting over the jam.

8   Store the cupcakes in an airtight container at room temperature for up to 3 days.

DEVIL'S FOOD CUPCAKES

1½ cups (213 grams) all-purpose flour

1½ cups (340 grams) sugar

½ cup (57 grams) unsweetened cocoa powder

1¼ teaspoons baking soda

¾ teaspoon salt

1 cup (225 milliliters) buttermilk

⅓ cup (71 milliliters) vegetable oil

½ cup (115 milliliters) strong brewed coffee, cooled

2 large eggs

1 teaspoon pure vanilla extract

1 recipe Chocolate Fudge Buttercream Frosting (page 276)

Sprinkles, for decorating (optional)

Buttermilk makes these cupcakes really moist, gives them an added layer of flavor, and keeps them from being too sweet. And if you use Dutch-process cocoa powder, these festive cupcakes will be a deep dark brown color and look amazing. The Chocolate Fudge Buttercream Frosting has been topped with colorful sprinkles, but it can be embellished with shaved chocolate for a more elegant look.

1   Preheat the oven to 350°F (180°C). Line two cupcake pans with 20 paper liners.

2   In a large bowl, mix together the flour, sugar, cocoa powder, baking soda, and salt.

3   In a medium bowl or large measuring cup, whisk together the buttermilk, oil, coffee, eggs, and vanilla.

4   Slowly whisk the buttermilk mixture into the flour mixture until just incorporated.

5   Divide the batter among the prepared cupcake pans, filling each well three-quarters full.

6   Bake for 15 to 18 minutes, until a toothpick inserted into the center of a cupcake comes out clean. These cupcakes bake very quickly. Let the cupcakes cool in the pans on a wire rack for 20 minutes, then turn them out onto the rack to cool completely.

7   Decorate the cupcakes with a swirl of frosting and some sprinkles, if desired. Enjoy straight away or store in an airtight container at room temperature for up to 3 days.

NOTE

This is also the ultimate chocolate cake recipe. Divide the batter between two greased 9-inch round cake pans and bake for 25 to 28 minutes, until a toothpick inserted into the center of the cakes comes out clean. Use Chocolate Fudge Buttercream Frosting to frost the cake. You're welcome . . .

CONFETTI CUPCAKES

MAKES 12 CUPCAKES

1⅔ cups (236 grams) all-purpose flour

½ teaspoon baking powder

¼ teaspoon baking soda

½ teaspoon salt

½ cup (1 stick/ 115 grams) butter, melted

¾ cup (170 grams) granulated sugar

¼ cup (43 grams) light brown sugar

1 large egg

1 cup (225 milliliters) buttermilk

1 tablespoon pure vanilla extract

3 tablespoons sprinkles, plus more for decorating

1 recipe Birthday Cake Buttercream Frosting (page 276)

Until my friend Suzie got me one for my birthday, I had never experienced the festive beauty of a confetti cake. After one bite, I was hooked. I knew confetti cake would make great cupcakes, too, so I made it my mission to create the prettiest, most delicious confetti cupcakes possible. Kids (of any age!) will love these—they are heaped with Birthday Cake Buttercream Frosting and each is festooned with a generous helping of colorful confetti sprinkles on top.

1   Preheat the oven to 350°F (180°C). Line a 12-cup cupcake pan with paper liners.

2   In a large bowl, mix together the flour, baking powder, baking soda, and salt.

3   In a medium bowl, combine the melted butter and sugars and whisk vigorously to break up any lumps. Stir in the egg, buttermilk, and vanilla until combined.

4   Slowly mix the dry ingredients into the wet ingredients until no lumps remain. Add the sprinkles and stir briefly to combine; do not overmix, or the sprinkles will bleed their color.

5   Spoon the batter into the prepared pan, filling the cups almost to the top.

6   Bake for 25 to 30 minutes, until the cupcakes are firm to the touch on top. Turn the cupcakes out of the pan and set them on a wire rack to cool completely.

7   Decorate the cupcakes with a swirl of birthday cake frosting on top and add a few extra sprinkles for color. Store at room temperature in an airtight container for up to 3 days.

BAKED BLUEBERRY CHEESECAKE

MAKES 12 SERVINGS

2⅓ cups (198 grams/
18 cookies) graham
cracker crumbs

6 tablespoons (¾ stick/
85 grams) butter,
melted

4½ cups (36 ounces/
1,015 grams) cream
cheese, softened

1 cup (225 grams) sugar

1 tablespoon pure vanilla
extract

Grated zest and juice of
1 lemon

5 large eggs, at room
temperature

¼ cup (35 grams)
all-purpose flour

2½ cups (355 grams)
blueberries

Whipped cream,
for serving

People who are obsessed with cheesecake will love this take on the traditional version. It has the usual graham cracker crust, cream cheese filling, and blueberries. But instead of putting berries on the top, I stir them into the filling. It's quite pretty with the blueberries in a violet swirl throughout. This will quickly become your go-to cheesecake.

1   Preheat the oven to 350°F (180°C).

2   In a medium bowl, mix together the cookie crumbs and melted butter. Press the crumb mixture into the bottom of a 9-inch springform pan. Refrigerate for 30 minutes to set.

3   Using a stand mixer or a handheld electric mixer, beat the cream cheese and sugar on high speed until smooth.

4   Add the vanilla, lemon zest, and lemon juice and beat to combine.

5   Add the eggs, one at a time, mixing each until fully blended before adding the next. At this point, your cream cheese mixture should be nice and airy from all the mixing.

6   Add the flour and mix until just combined. Fold in the blueberries.

7   Pour the batter on top of your cookie base.

8   Bake for about 1 hour 40 minutes, until the cheesecake is set but still jiggles slightly in the middle. If it is getting too brown on top, cover it with aluminum foil. Set the pan on a wire rack and let cool completely, then refrigerate the cheesecake, still in the pan, for a few hours to firm up.

9   Serve with whipped cream. Store in the fridge, covered, for up to 4 days.

NO-BAKE OREO CHEESECAKE

MAKES 12 SERVINGS

FOR THE CRUST

2½ cups (213 grams/
33 cookies) Oreo cookie
crumbs (see Note)

7 tablespoons
(99 grams) butter,
melted

FOR THE FILLING

3 cups (24 ounces/
675 grams) cream
cheese, softened

⅔ cup (142 grams) sugar

2 teaspoons pure vanilla
extract

2¼ cups (507 milliliters)
heavy cream

1½ cups (135 grams/
20 cookies) crushed
Oreo cookies (see Note)

1 recipe Rich Chocolate
Ganache (page 284),
warm enough to be
pourable

This cheesecake is one of my most beloved recipes, and one reason may be because it's so big, making it a huge crowd-pleaser. I've used Oreos two ways here—crushed to create the crust, and mixed into the cream cheese filling. And maybe the best part? No baking! All you need to do is assemble everything in the pan and chill it for at least 8 hours before serving.

1 *To make the cheesecake base:* In a medium bowl, combine the cookie crumbs and the melted butter and mix well. Press the mixture over the bottom of a 9-inch springform pan. Refrigerate for 30 minutes to set.

2 *To make the cheesecake filling:* Using a stand mixer fitted with the paddle attachment, or a handheld electric mixer, beat the cream cheese, sugar, and vanilla on high speed until smooth and free of lumps, approximately 3 to 5 minutes. Run a spatula under the mix to make sure there are no cream cheese lumps.

3 Pour in the cream and beat until the mixture becomes very thick.

4 Gently fold in the crushed cookies.

5 Pour the cheesecake filling over the crust. Tap the pan on the countertop to level the filling and release any air bubbles.

6 Pour a thick layer of chocolate ganache over the surface of the cheesecake in the pan.

7 Refrigerate for at least 8 hours to set, or preferably overnight for best results.

8 Store in the refrigerator, covered, for up to 4 days.

NOTE

Remove the creme center from the Oreos before you crush them—you only need the cookies themselves. Alternatively, you could substitute another brand of chocolate wafer cookies, such as Nabisco Famous Chocolate Wafers.

FLOURLESS CHOCOLATE CAKE

MAKES 8 SERVINGS

1⅓ cups (8 ounces/ 225 grams) chopped bittersweet chocolate

1 cup (2 sticks/ 225 grams) butter

1¼ cups (282 grams) sugar

1 teaspoon pure vanilla extract

6 large eggs, at room temperature, separated

1 cup (115 grams) unsweetened cocoa powder

½ teaspoon salt

Vanilla ice cream, for serving

1 recipe Rich Chocolate Ganache (page 284), warm enough to be pourable

Really rich and satisfying, this absolutely delicious flourless cake is ideal for anyone sensitive to gluten, but anyone with a craving for chocolate will love it, too. If you are going to an event and aren't sure if any of the guests are gluten-free, bring this. The addition of Rich Chocolate Ganache, a chocolate lover's dream, makes this spectacular.

1   Preheat the oven to 350°F (180°C). Grease a 9-inch springform pan and line it with parchment paper.

2   Put the chocolate and butter in a large bowl and melt them together in the microwave or over a bain-marie (see page 30). Let cool for 10 minutes.

3   Whisk in the sugar and the vanilla. Add the egg yolks, one at a time, and whisk to incorporate.

4   Sift the cocoa powder and salt over the chocolate mixture and whisk to combine.

5   Using a stand mixer fitted with the whisk attachment, or handheld electric mixer, whip the egg whites on medium-high speed until stiff peaks form.

6   Gently fold a large spoonful of the egg whites into the chocolate mixture to loosen it, then gently fold in the rest of the egg whites, taking care not to deflate the egg whites.

7   Pour the batter into the prepared pan.

8   Bake for 40 to 45 minutes, until set on top. Take care not to overbake, or the cake won't be as moist. Let cool in the pan for 40 minutes.

9   Serve warm, topped with a big scoop of vanilla ice cream and a drizzle of chocolate ganache. Store at room temperature, covered, for up to 3 days.

30-MINUTE CHOCOLATE ROULADE

MAKES 8 SERVINGS

6 large eggs, at room temperature, separated

⅔ cup (142 grams) sugar

½ cup (57 grams) unsweetened cocoa powder, plus more for dusting

1½ cups (340 milliliters) heavy cream

½ recipe Three-Ingredient Chocolate Mousse (page 231)

A roulade is a very thin cake that is rolled up with layers of mousse and whipped cream and cut into slices. The cake is usually a bit squidgy (which is just my way of saying it's light and soft)—just what you want to make it easy to roll up without breaking or cracking. When I was younger and living at home, my mum would ask me to make this for her dinner parties, and I was quite proud that she thought I could make something nice enough to serve to guests. In fact, when I was about twelve years old, Mum asked me to make one for a neighbor who had just had a baby. The woman quizzed me about the recipe in great detail because she didn't believe someone so young could have made something so sophisticated. It *is* rather impressive looking, but it's not nearly as hard as it looks.

1   Preheat the oven to 350°F (180°C). Grease a 10 x 15-inch rimmed baking sheet and line it with parchment paper.

2   Using a stand mixer fitted with the whisk attachment or a handheld electric mixer, whip the egg yolks and sugar on high speed until thick and fluffy.

3   Sift the cocoa powder over the egg mixture and then fold it in with a large metal spoon.

4   In a clean mixer bowl using a clean whisk attachment, whip the egg whites until stiff peaks form.

5   Carefully fold the egg whites into the chocolate mixture.

6   Pour the batter into the prepared pan and spread it evenly with a spatula.

7   Bake for 20 to 25 minutes, until the top of the cake is firm to the touch. Let the cake cool in the pan for 5 minutes,

then, while the cake is still warm, remove it from the pan and roll it up lengthwise (this stops the cake from cracking when you go to roll it again later). Let the rolled cake cool completely.

8 Meanwhile, whip the cream until stiff peaks form.

9 Unroll the cooled cake and spread with a layer of chocolate mousse, leaving a 1-inch border exposed. Top the mousse with an even layer of whipped cream.

10 Carefully roll up the cake and transfer it to a serving platter, seam-side down.

11 Dust with cocoa powder and serve nice thick slices. Keep refrigerated, covered, for up to 3 days.

RED VELVET CAKE
WITH CREAM CHEESE FROSTING

MAKES 12 SERVINGS

2½ cups (355 grams) all-purpose flour

1½ cups (340 grams) sugar

1 teaspoon ground cinnamon

3 tablespoons unsweetened cocoa powder

1½ teaspoons baking soda

1 teaspoon salt

2 large eggs

1½ cups (340 milliliters) vegetable oil

1 cup (225 milliliters) buttermilk

¼ cup (57 milliliters) red food coloring

2 teaspoons pure vanilla extract

1 recipe Cream Cheese Frosting (page 279)

NOTE

If your cakes have a domed top, you can level them with a serrated knife to make them nice and even.

When I first moved to the US, I tried lots of American recipes to help me acclimate to the local culture. I loved everything about red velvet cake—its indulgent cream cheese frosting and the "surprise" when you cut a slice and discover the intense red of the cake. This recipe stays close to the classic, with two round cake layers and thick, creamy frosting covering everything, because why change something that is already practically perfect?

1 Preheat the oven to 350°F (180°C). Grease two 9-inch round cake pans and line them with parchment paper.

2 Sift together the flour, sugar, cinnamon, cocoa powder, baking soda, and salt into a large bowl.

3 In a large measuring cup, whisk together the eggs, oil, buttermilk, food coloring, and vanilla.

4 Whisk the wet ingredients into the dry ingredients (take care not to overmix the batter as overmixing can toughen the cake).

5 Divide the batter evenly between the prepared pans.

6 Bake for 30 to 35 minutes, until a toothpick inserted into the center of each cake comes out clean. Let the cakes cool in the pans on a wire rack for 20 minutes, then turn them out onto the rack to cool completely.

7 To assemble the cake, place one cake layer on a flat serving plate or cake pedestal (see Note). Put a dollop of frosting in the center of the cake. With an offset spatula,

RECIPE CONTINUES

spread it all the way to the edges of the cake, creating an even layer of frosting. Top with the second cake layer. Spread another big dollop of frosting on top. Work the frosting over the top and then down the sides, roughly covering the cake with a thin layer of frosting. (This step is just the first layer, known as the crumb coat. Don't worry, it's not supposed to be beautiful.)

8   Refrigerate the cake for at least 30 minutes to set the crumb coat. (This will make the finished cake look really clean, I promise.)

9   Take the cake out of the fridge and dollop the remaining frosting on top. Spread the frosting over down the sides to cover the whole cake. Try to get it as smooth as you can. You shouldn't have any red crumbs floating around in the frosting, but some might sneak in.

10 This is an elegant cake, so I decorate it simply, with some fresh edible flowers on top. Keep the cake at room temperature, covered, for up to 4 days.

CLASSIC **COCONUT CAKE**

1 cup (2 sticks/ 225 grams) butter, softened

2 cups (450 grams) sugar

4 large eggs, separated

1½ teaspoons coconut extract (see page 300 to make your own)

2 cups (284 grams) all-purpose flour

1 teaspoon baking soda

4⅓ cups (370 grams) unsweetened shredded coconut

1 cup (225 milliliters) buttermilk

1 recipe Cream Cheese Frosting (page 279)

Coconut is one of my favorite ingredients—and this traditional coconut cake is a stunning way to use it. The cake has both shredded coconut and coconut extract in the batter, which gives it a nice intense flavor. Then it gets a generous coating of fluffy Cream Cheese Frosting. Finally, lots of shredded coconut is pressed into the frosting for decoration, making the cake absolutely gorgeous.

1 Preheat the oven to 350°F (180°C). Grease two 9-inch round cake pans and line them with parchment paper.

2 Using a stand mixer fitted with the paddle attachment, or a handheld electric mixer, beat the butter and sugar on high speed until light and fluffy. Beat in the egg yolks and coconut extract.

3 In a medium bowl, stir together the flour, baking soda, and 1⅓ cups (115 grams) of the coconut.

4 With the mixer on low speed, add the flour mixture and the buttermilk, in alternating batches, until fully combined, scraping down the sides of the bowl as needed.

5 In a medium bowl, whisk the egg whites until stiff peaks form. Gently fold the egg whites into the coconut mixture.

6 Divide the batter evenly between the prepared pans.

7 Bake for 30 to 35 minutes, until a toothpick inserted into the center comes clean. Let the cakes cool in the pans for 5 minutes, then turn them out onto a wire rack to cool completely.

RECIPE CONTINUES

8   *To assemble the cake:* Place one cake layer on a flat serving plate or cake pedestal. Spread some cream cheese frosting on the top all the way to the edges of the cake. Top with the second cake layer and spread the remaining frosting evenly over the top and down the sides of the cake.

9   Gently use the palm of your hand to press the remaining 3 cups (255 grams) shredded coconut onto the sides and top of the cake, covering it completely.

10 Store at room temperature, covered, for up to 4 days.

STRAWBERRY & CREAM
SPONGE CAKE

MAKES 12 SERVINGS

1 cup (2 sticks/
225 grams) butter,
softened

1 cup (225 grams) sugar

4 large eggs, beaten

1⅔ cups (225 grams)
self-rising flour
(see page 304)

1 teaspoon baking
powder

2 tablespoons whole
milk

¾ cup (170 milliliters)
heavy cream

1½ cups (213 grams)
strawberries, sliced

Confectioners' sugar,
for decorating

This is the Irish equivalent of an American yellow cake; some know it as a Victoria sponge. Almost every house I went to when I was growing up would serve this with a cup of tea. The sponge cake layers take only 20 minutes to bake, and decorating is a snap: I place strawberries in a decorative pattern over one of the sponge cakes and then top them with a thick layer of whipped cream. Then, after adding the second cake layer, I dust the top of the cake with confectioners' sugar. (For an especially pretty finish, I like to place a doily on top of the cake before dusting it with the sugar.) That's it! It's simple to make and tastes so good.

1   Preheat the oven to 350°F (180°C). Grease two 9-inch round cake pans and line them with parchment paper.

2   In a large bowl, cream together the butter and sugar until fluffy and pale in color.

3   One by one, slowly incorporate the eggs and beat until well combined.

4   Add the flour, baking powder, and milk and fold in gently until you have a smooth batter.

5   Divide the batter between the prepared pans and smooth the tops with a spatula.

RECIPE CONTINUES

6   Bake for 20 to 25 minutes, until the cake is golden and springs back when pressed. Let the cakes cool in the pans on a wire rack for 20 minutes, then turn them out onto the rack to cool completely.

7   *To assemble the cake:* Whip the cream until stiff peaks form.

8   Set one cake layer bottom-side down on a serving plate or cake pedestal. Arrange the strawberries over the cake, top with the whipped cream, and sandwich the second cake layer on top.

9   Dust generously with confectioners' sugar before serving. Keep in the fridge, covered, for up to 3 days.

BLACK FOREST GÂTEAU

MAKES 12 SERVINGS

FOR THE MACERATED CHERRIES

2 cups (12 ounces/ 340 grams) cherries, pitted

¼ cup (57 milliliters) Kirsch or other fruit brandy

¼ cup (57 grams) granulated sugar

FOR THE DEVIL'S FOOD CAKE

1½ cups (213 grams) all-purpose flour

1½ cups (340 grams) granulated sugar

½ cup (57 grams) unsweetened cocoa powder

1¼ teaspoons baking soda

¾ teaspoon salt

1 cup (225 milliliters) buttermilk

⅓ cup (71 milliliters) vegetable oil

½ cup (115 milliliters) strong brewed coffee, cooled

2 large eggs

1 teaspoon pure vanilla extract

Cherries and chocolate are wonderful together and star in this classic German cake. Black Forest Gâteau was popular back in the 1970s, but it's such a pretty and delicious cake that I think it deserves to come back in style. Dark chocolate cake is layered with mascarpone cream and a fresh cherry sauce. Then chocolate ganache is poured over the top and the cake is garnished with more cherries and shaved chocolate curls. This one is special enough to celebrate a birthday or an anniversary.

1. *To make the macerated cherries:* In a small bowl, mix the cherries, Kirsch, and sugar. Set aside to macerate at room temperature for at least 2 hours or, preferably, overnight in the fridge.

2. *To make the cake:* Preheat the oven to 350°F (180°C). Grease two 9-inch cake pans and line them with parchment paper.

3. In a large bowl, mix together the flour, sugar, cocoa powder, baking soda, and salt.

4. In a medium bowl or large measuring cup, whisk together the buttermilk, oil, coffee, eggs, and vanilla.

5. Slowly whisk the buttermilk mixture into the flour mixture until just incorporated.

6. Divide the batter between the prepared pans.

7. Bake for 18 to 20 minutes, until a toothpick inserted into the center comes out clean. These cakes bake very quickly. Let the cakes cool in the pans for 20 minutes, then turn them out onto a wire rack to cool completely.

RECIPE AND INGREDIENTS CONTINUE

1 cup (225 grams) mascarpone cheese

¼ cup (28 grams) confectioners' sugar

¼ cup (57 milliliters) heavy cream

1 recipe Rich Chocolate Ganache (page 284)

3 whole cherries, for decorating

Chocolate shavings, for decorating (see page 21)

8   *To make the mascarpone cream:* Using a stand mixer fitted with the whisk attachment, or a handheld electric mixer, whip the mascarpone and confectioners' sugar together until smooth. Pour in the cream and whip until the mixture has thickened. Refrigerate until needed.

9   *To assemble the cake:* Place one cake layer on a flat serving platter or cake pedestal. Spread the mascarpone cream evenly over the top. Spoon over the macerated cherries and some of the juice. Set the second cake layer on top, pressing down gently to hold it in place.

10 To finish, pour the chocolate ganache over the top, letting it drip over the sides. Garnish with extra cherries and shave over some chocolate.

STRONG COFFEE & TOASTED WALNUT CAKE

MAKES 12 SERVINGS

2 tablespoons instant coffee granules

2 tablespoons boiling water

1 cup (2 sticks/ 225 grams) butter, softened

1 cup (225 grams) sugar

4 large eggs, beaten

1⅔ cups (225 grams) self-rising flour (see page 304)

1 teaspoon baking powder

1 cup (142 grams) plus 3 tablespoons walnuts, chopped and toasted

1 recipe Coffee Buttercream Frosting (page 276)

Most everyone has a favorite cake they wish for on their birthday. Mine is this light, spongelike cake thickly covered with buttercream, which has coffee in both the cake and the frosting. Every year for my birthday, I would ask for it, and my mum would buy one at the local bakery. I loved the texture of the chopped nuts in the cake and how the top was decorated with more walnuts. Today when I go home for a visit, my mum will have this cake ready for me when I arrive, only now she makes it for me from scratch, which is even better.

1 Preheat the oven to 350°F (180°C). Grease two 9-inch round cake pans and line them with parchment paper.

2 In a small bowl, combine the coffee granules and boiling water and stir until the coffee has dissolved. Set aside.

3 Using a stand mixer fitted with the paddle attachment, or a handheld electric mixer, cream together the butter and sugar until fluffy and pale in color.

4 One by one, slowly incorporate the eggs and mix until well combined.

5 Add the flour, baking powder, and dissolved coffee and carefully fold together until you have a smooth batter.

6 Fold in 1 cup (142 grams) of the walnuts.

7 Divide the batter between the prepared pans, smoothing the surface with a spoon.

RECIPE CONTINUES

8   Bake for 20 to 25 minutes, until the cake is firm on top and springs back when pressed. Let the cakes cool in the pans on a wire rack for 20 minutes, then turn them out onto the rack to cool completely.

9   To assemble the cake, place one cake layer on a serving plate or cake pedestal. Put a dollop of frosting in the center of the cake. With an offset spatula, spread it all the way to the edges of the cake, creating an even layer of frosting. Top with the second cake layer and spread another big dollop of frosting on top, smoothing it out with the spatula.

10 If you'd like, transfer some of the frosting to a piping bag fitted with a large star tip and pipe some rosettes on top of the cake.

11 Scatter over the remaining 3 tablespoons walnuts. Store the cake in an airtight container at room temperature for up to 4 days.

ALL-THE-SPRINKLES BIRTHDAY CAKE

MAKES 12 SERVINGS

1 large egg plus 5 large egg whites

1 cup (225 milliliters) buttermilk

2 teaspoons pure vanilla extract

3 cups (426 grams) cake flour, sifted

2 cups (450 grams) sugar

4 teaspoons baking powder

½ teaspoon salt

¾ cup (1½ sticks/ 170 grams) cold butter, cubed

1 recipe Vanilla Buttercream Frosting (page 276)

2 cups (454 grams) sprinkles, for decorating

Two layers are good, but three layers are even better, right? This is the ultimate birthday cake—vanilla cake with a classic buttercream frosting—but I'm not the best cake decorator, so I love to simply cover the cake in rainbow sprinkles, which are so festive and beautiful (and anyone can decorate a cake this way with great results). The three layers make it very tall, and it will surely be the centerpiece of any celebration.

1 Preheat the oven to 350°F (180°C). Grease three 6-inch cake pans and line them with parchment paper. (Alternatively, you could use two 8-inch cake pans.)

2 In a large measuring cup, whisk together the egg, egg whites, buttermilk, and vanilla. Set aside.

3 Using a stand mixer fitted with the paddle attachment or a handheld electric mixer, combine the flour, sugar, baking powder, and salt and beat on low speed for 1 minute. (You could also do this by hand using a wooden spoon.)

4 Add the butter and continue to mix on low speed until the mixture resembles coarse bread crumbs.

5 Add the wet ingredients to the dry ingredients in two batches, making sure to scrape the sides and bottom of the bowl in between. Mix until the batter is light, fluffy, and well incorporated.

6 Divide the batter evenly among the prepared pans.

7 Bake for 40 to 45 minutes, until a toothpick inserted into the center of the cake comes out clean. Let the cakes cool in the pans on wire racks for 20 minutes, then turn them out onto the racks to cool completely. (If you are not

RECIPE CONTINUES

If your cakes have some knobbly bits, don't worry—just trim the layers with a serrated knife so all your layers are even.

If you'd like, you can reserve a little frosting in a piping bag fitted with a large star tip, then pipe some rosettes on top of the cake after applying the sprinkles.

assembling the cake right away, wrap the cooled layers tightly in plastic wrap and store at room temperature for up to 2 days.)

8   To assemble the cake, place one cake layer on a flat serving plate or cake pedestal. Spread frosting all over the top with a small offset spatula. Top with the second cake layer and repeat with more frosting.

9   Top with the third cake layer. Add a generous dollop of frosting on top and spread evenly, working your way over the top and down the sides until you have a thin layer of frosting over the entire cake. This is called the "crumb layer" and will prevent crumbs from ending up in the final frosting.

10 Refrigerate the cake for at least 30 minutes to set the crumb coat.

11 Take the cake out of the fridge and apply a final layer of frosting all over the cake (see Note).

12 To apply the sprinkles: Place the cake on a large baking sheet before decorating to catch your excess sprinkles. Pour the sprinkles over the top of the cake, then use your hand to press them into the sides of the cake. Just keep on applying them until they stick all over.

13 Store in an airtight container at room temperature for up to 3 days.

Chapter 5

MIXER

AS A GIRL, I STARTED BAKING WITH JUST A SPOON and a bowl, but once I gained some skills, I was allowed to use an electric mixer. My mum had a lovely stand mixer that she used for whipping egg whites to make pavlova for dinner parties and mixing ingredients to make cakes. When the stand mixer was working really hard on a stiff batter, it tended to hop around on the counter, and once, when I was using it, it hopped right off and crashed to the floor. It still worked after that—that mixer must be indestructible—and I never told my mum. She still uses it today. Years later, when I had my catering business, I had very little money but I carefully saved up to buy a KitchenAid mixer. It was one of the few pieces of equipment I owned. I loved that they came in so many lovely colors, and once I finally bought one for myself (mine is candy apple red!), I felt like I was truly an adult.

STICKY TOFFEE PUDDING

MAKES 22 PUDDINGS

2⅓ cups (350 grams) pitted dates

2⅓ cups (530 milliliters) water

2 teaspoons baking soda

7 tablespoons (99 grams) butter, softened

1½ cups (340 grams) light brown sugar

4 large eggs, at room temperature

2⅓ cups (311 grams) self-rising flour (see page 304)

2 teaspoons pure vanilla extract

My Signature Salted Caramel Sauce (page 288), for serving

Vanilla ice cream, for serving

This pudding, which gets its moist and light texture from finely chopped dates, is a staple on dessert menus all over Ireland. I bake it in a cupcake tin for individual puddings that look special and are perfect for company. It can be topped with vanilla ice cream and/or My Signature Salted Caramel Sauce, and I encourage you to serve it warm, which is most traditional and, I think, the best way to enjoy it.

1 Preheat the oven to 350°F (180°C). Butter two 12-cup cupcake pans.

2 In a medium saucepan, combine the dates and water, cover, and bring to a boil over medium heat. Reduce the heat and simmer for 5 to 8 minutes, until the dates are soft. Remove from the heat.

3 Add the baking soda to the hot date mixture to activate it; it will fizz up. Set aside for 20 minutes to cool.

4 Transfer the date mixture to a food processor and blend into a smooth paste.

5 Using a stand mixer fitted with the paddle attachment, or a handheld electric mixer, cream together the butter and brown sugar until light and fluffy.

6 Add the eggs, one at a time, and mix until fully incorporated.

7 Stir in the flour and vanilla.

8 Pour in the cooled date mixture and mix until just combined.

9 Divide the batter among the prepared cupcake pans, filling 22 of the wells three-quarters full.

10 Bake for 20 to 22 minutes, until the puddings are firm on top.

11 Enjoy warm, with caramel sauce and vanilla ice cream. Let any leftover puddings cool completely, then store in an airtight container at room temperature for up to 4 days.

STEAMED BANANA PUDDING

¾ cup (1½ sticks/
170 grams) butter,
softened

¾ cup (170 grams) sugar

4 large eggs, at room
temperature

¾ cup (170 grams)
almond flour or
almond meal

⅔ cup (94 grams)
all-purpose flour

1½ teaspoons baking
powder

2 medium bananas,
mashed

1 recipe My Signature
Salted Caramel Sauce
(page 288), for serving

Whipped cream,
for serving

In Ireland, "pudding" is unlike what you might find in America. It's more like an extremely moist cake (often cooked by steaming) than a creamy, mousse-like dessert. Believe me, though, it's just as comforting. As you might imagine, I adore this version even more because of my love for bananas. It's too bad I didn't start making this with bananas until I was an adult—I would have loved the gooey sweetness of this dessert after a Sunday meal when I was a kid.

1 Place a steamer basket in a large, deep saucepan. Fill the pan with water until it touches the bottom of the basket. Bring the water to a simmer.

2 Using a stand mixer fitted with the paddle attachment, or a handheld electric mixer, cream together the butter and sugar until light and pale in color.

3 Add the eggs one by one and beat until incorporated.

4 Add the almond flour, all-purpose flour, baking powder, and banana and mix until combined.

5 Pour the pudding batter into a large (2-quart/2-liter) pudding mold or bowl that will fit inside the saucepan and steamer and cover tightly with plastic wrap (I wrap the whole bowl a few times).

6 Set the bowl in the steamer, cover, and reduce the heat to medium-low. Steam the pudding for about 2 hours, until it is firm in the middle. Keep an eye on the water level in the saucepan and add water as needed if it gets low.

7 Remove the plastic wrap and turn the pudding out onto a plate.

8 Serve warm, with the caramel sauce and whipped cream.

WINTER APPLE EVE'S PUDDING

5 medium apples, such as Granny Smith or Bramley, peeled, cored, and coarsely chopped into 1-inch pieces (about 8 cups/900 grams)

¾ cup (172 grams) sugar

½ cup (1 stick/ 115 grams) butter, softened

2 large eggs, at room temperature

¾ cup (115 grams) self-rising flour (see page 304)

2 tablespoons whole milk

Vanilla ice cream, for serving

In Ireland, it's common to stew apples until they pretty much disintegrate into applesauce, probably because the apple variety most available to home cooks is the Bramley, which is too tart to eat out of hand. Eve's pudding makes great use of Bramleys, which lose their intense sourness when baked and create a luscious, puddinglike texture. Topped with a layer of tender Victoria sponge cake, each bite is a wonderful mix of tangy and sweet. If you can't find Bramleys, try an apple like Granny Smith or McIntosh to get close to the very soft consistency that makes this dessert so enticing.

1   Preheat the oven to 350°F (180°C).

2   Place the apples in a 9-inch baking dish and stir in ¼ cup (57 grams) of the sugar to coat.

3   Using a stand mixer fitted with the paddle attachment, or a handheld electric mixer, cream together the butter and remaining ½ cup (115 grams) sugar until pale and fluffy.

4   Add the eggs one a time and mix until incorporated.

5   Fold in the flour, followed by the milk.

6   Pour the batter over the apples in the baking dish.

7   Bake for 50 minutes to 1 hour, until the top of the cake is browned.

8   Serve hot, with vanilla ice cream. Store leftovers in the fridge, covered, for up to 3 days.

STAFFORD'S PINEAPPLE UPSIDE-DOWN CAKE

MAKES 8 SERVINGS

¾ cup (1½ sticks/ 170 grams) butter, softened

½ cup (85 grams) light brown sugar

6 pineapple rings

11 maraschino cherries

½ cup (115 grams) granulated sugar

2 large eggs, at room temperature

1 teaspoon pure vanilla extract

¾ cup (115 grams) self-rising flour (see page 304)

The classic pineapple upside-down cake went out of style years ago, but it's making a big comeback. I'm sure most of you remember the pineapple and cherries, coated with a caramel sauce, that made this cake so irresistible. This is a great last-minute dessert because it comes together very quickly. Serve it warm, with dollops of whipped cream or scoops of vanilla ice cream, or on its own, with a cup of tea.

1. Preheat the oven to 350°F (180°C). Smear 4 tablespoons (½ stick/57 grams) of the butter over the bottom and up the sides of a 9-inch round cake pan. Coat the surface generously with the brown sugar.

2. Lay the pineapple rings in the cake pan. Place the cherries in the centers and in between the rings.

3. Using a stand mixer fitted with the paddle attachment, or a handheld electric mixer, cream together the remaining ½ cup (1 stick/115 grams) butter and the granulated sugar until light and fluffy.

4. Add the eggs, one at a time, and mix until incorporated. Add the vanilla and mix to combine.

5. Sift the flour over the mixer bowl and gently fold it in with a large metal spoon until just combined.

6. Pour the batter over the pineapple in the prepared pan.

7. Bake for 40 to 45 minutes, until the cake feels firm to the touch in the middle. Let cool in the pan for 5 minutes, then turn the cake out onto a serving platter.

8. Store leftovers in an airtight container at room temperature for up to 3 days.

SIMPLEST VANILLA SWISS ROLL

MAKES 6 TO 8 SERVINGS

4 large eggs, at room temperature

⅔ cup (142 grams) granulated sugar

2 teaspoons pure vanilla extract

1 cup (142 grams) all-purpose flour

¾ cup (213 grams) strawberry jam

1½ cup (340 milliliters) heavy cream

Confectioners' sugar, for dusting

The ultimate in simplicity, the Swiss roll is a very light and airy cake that is rolled up with jam—most commonly strawberry—and whipped cream. My mum would always make it from scratch, though many people would buy them at bakeries and have them ready in case someone dropped by for tea. It's lovely when it's cut into slices, and once you get the hang of rolling up the cake, you'll see how easy it is to make. Serve with tea and some friendly banter.

1   Preheat the oven to 350°F (180°C). Grease a 10 x 15-inch rimmed baking sheet and line it with parchment paper.

2   Using a stand mixer fitted with the whisk attachment, or a handheld electric mixer, whisk the eggs, granulated sugar, and vanilla on high speed until very fluffy and thickened, around 5 to 8 minutes (it's really important to get it thick).

3   Sift the flour over the mixture and fold it in very gently with a large, thin-edged spoon, taking care not to knock out the air in the bubbles you made by whisking.

4   Pour the batter into the prepared baking sheet and smooth the top evenly with a spatula.

5   Bake for 10 to 12 minutes, until firm to the touch. This cake bakes very fast.

6   Immediately turn the cake out of the pan onto a clean kitchen towel. Remove the parchment paper and then gently roll up the warm cake lengthwise in the towel. Let cool completely (this prevents the cake from cracking when it's rolled again later).

7   Meanwhile, whip the cream until stiff peaks form.

8 Unroll the cake. Spread the strawberry jam all over the cake, leaving a ½-inch border around the edges. Spread a layer of the whipped cream over the jam.

9 Roll the cake up carefully, removing the towel as you go. Transfer it to a serving plate, seam side down.

10 To serve, dust with confectioners' sugar. Keep refrigerated, covered, for up to 2 days.

AFTERNOON TEA LINZER TORTE

MAKES 10 SERVINGS

½ cup (1 stick/ 115 grams) butter, softened

½ cup (115 grams) sugar

3 large eggs plus 1 large egg yolk

1⅓ cups (185 grams) all-purpose flour

2½ cups (283 grams) almond flour or almond meal

2 teaspoons ground cinnamon

2 teaspoons ground cloves

1 tablespoon grated lemon zest

1 teaspoon baking powder

½ cup (142 grams) raspberry jam

¼ cup (35 grams) sliced almonds

When I worked as a chef at a spa back in Ireland, I would make this delicious cake in the afternoon, baking it in gigantic trays and cutting it into perfect squares, leaving scraps that the other kitchen workers would then sneak when they could get a chance. The version I make at home now is round, leaving no extra pieces for hungry fingers. The dense almond-flavored cake goes well with whatever jam you use, although raspberry is traditional.

1   Preheat the oven to 350°F (180°C). Grease a 9-inch round cake pan and line it with parchment paper.

2   Using a stand mixer fitted with the paddle attachment, or a handheld electric mixer, cream together the butter and sugar until fluffy and pale in color.

3   Add the eggs and the egg yolk, one at a time, and mix until well combined.

4   In a medium bowl, stir together the all-purpose flour, almond flour, cinnamon, cloves, lemon zest, and baking powder.

5   Add the dry ingredients to the wet ingredients and mix until just combined.

6   Spread three-quarters of the batter over the bottom of your prepared pan and smooth it down with a spatula. Spread the jam over the batter.

7   Fill a piping bag fitted with a medium round tip with the rest of the cake batter and pipe a lattice pattern over the jam layer. Scatter sliced almonds around the edge of the cake and press them lightly to adhere.

8   Bake for 30 to 35 minutes, until golden brown on top. Let cool completely. Store in an airtight container at room temperature for up to 3 days.

MERINGUE ROULADE WITH BANANAS & SALTED CARAMEL SAUCE

MAKES 8 SERVINGS

5 large egg whites, at room temperature

1¼ cups (282 grams) granulated sugar

2 cups (450 milliliters) heavy cream

3 medium bananas, thinly sliced

1 recipe My Signature Salted Caramel Sauce (page 288)

Confectioners' sugar, for decorating

One of my favorite desserts is a meringue roulade, which is very common in Ireland: Instead of using cake as in a traditional roulade, meringue is rolled up with whipped cream and fruit. I've made this for many a party and catering job to much acclaim, particularly in the US, because it's not well-known here. After being struck by inspiration one day, I filled the meringue with bananas and then poured caramel sauce over the top. It was divine and literally melted in my mouth. I have unapologetically eaten this whole thing by myself on at least one occasion, and I'll probably do it again.

1 Preheat the oven to 350°F (180°C). Grease a 10 x 15-inch rimmed baking sheet and line it with parchment paper.

2 Using a stand mixer fitted with the whisk attachment, or a handheld electric mixer, whisk the egg whites on low speed for about 2 minutes, until they start to foam.

3 Increase the speed to medium-high and whip until the egg whites thicken and double in volume.

4 With the mixer running, gradually add the granulated sugar, 1 tablespoon at a time, and beat until the meringue is stiff and shiny. Once all the sugar has been added, whip for 2 minutes more.

5 Spread the meringue evenly over the prepared baking sheet.

6 Bake for about 20 minutes, until the meringue is slightly firm to touch on top but still soft inside. Set aside in the pan to cool completely .

RECIPE CONTINUES

7   Meanwhile, whip the cream until stiff peaks form. Set aside.

8   Lay a clean kitchen towel over the cooled meringue. Place a wire rack on top of the towel and, holding the rack and baking sheet together, flip them over. The baking sheet will be facing you now—lift it away and gently slide the rack out from underneath the roulade.

9   Carefully peel off the parchment paper. Don't worry if there are some holes in the meringue—they'll be covered by the whipped cream.

10 Spread the whipped cream all over the surface of the meringue (the side that had the parchment paper on it). Scatter the banana slices all over the cream and then drizzle with some salted caramel sauce.

11 Using the kitchen towel as your guide, gently roll up the meringue lengthwise like a jelly roll, enclosing the filling. Place the roulade on a serving platter, seam side down.

12 Dust liberally with confectioners' sugar (to cover any cracks) and drizzle with even more caramel sauce, if you wish. Store in the fridge, covered, for up to 2 days.

MUM'S FANCY PAVLOVA

MAKES 8 TO 10 SERVINGS

FOR THE MERINGUE

4 large egg whites (160 grams), at room temperature

1 cup (225 grams) sugar

2 teaspoons cornstarch

1 teaspoon distilled white vinegar

TO ASSEMBLE

1½ cups (340 milliliters) heavy cream

20 strawberries, sliced

3 kiwifruit, peeled and sliced

1 passion fruit, halved

Pavlovas, airy meringues topped with whipped cream and fruit, were one of the desserts my mum would make for dinner parties. I thought they were the height of sophistication. And with billowing mounds of whipped cream and the gorgeous colors of strawberries, kiwis, and passion fruit on top, my mum's pavlovas were the absolute best. She would let one of us help her make the meringue—crispy on the outside, fluffy and marshmallow-like on the inside— by giving the volunteer the sugar bowl and a spoon with instructions to wait patiently by the mixer. At the proper moment, Mum would instruct the bearer of the sugar bowl to add spoonfuls of sugar, one at a time, to the egg whites as they whipped up high. We knew that the kid who helped would be given the whisk to lick, so Mum never lacked an assistant. If we were very lucky, there would be leftovers and we would all be allowed to eat them the next day. It was heaven, and this is still one of my favorite desserts today.

1   *To make the meringue:* Preheat the oven to 275°F (135°C). Line a cookie sheet with parchment paper.

2   Using a stand mixer fitted with the whisk attachment, or a handheld electric mixer, whip the egg whites on low speed for 2 minutes, or until bubbles start to form.

3   Increase the speed to medium-high speed and whip until the egg whites start to thicken, roughly 2 to 3 minutes.

4   With the mixer running, slowly add the sugar, 1 tablespoon at a time, until it is all incorporated. The egg whites will double in volume and become shiny.

RECIPE CONTINUES

5   Add the cornstarch and vinegar and mix for 2 minutes more.

6   Spread the meringue into a 10-inch round on the prepared cookie sheet. Make a dip in the middle (this is where you will spread the cream).

7   Bake for 1¼ hours. Turn off the oven but leave the meringue in the oven to dry out for 3 hours.

8   *To assemble the pavlova:* Whip the cream until stiff peaks form. You can do this with a whisk by hand or using an electric mixer.

9   Spread the whipped cream over the meringue and top with the strawberries, kiwi, and passion fruit pulp. Store leftovers in the refrigerator, covered, for up to 2 days.

CHOCOLATE MERINGUE LAYER CAKE

6 large (240 grams) egg whites, at room temperature

2 cups (450 grams) sugar

2½ teaspoons cornstarch

1 teaspoon distilled white vinegar

3 tablespoons unsweetened cocoa powder, sifted

2 cups (450 milliliters) heavy cream

½ recipe Three-Ingredient Chocolate Mousse (page 231)

Chocolate shavings, for decorating (see page 21)

A chocolate cake made with layers of crispy meringue and mousse? I'll bet I had you at chocolate, right? This is a dramatic cake that's a bit different from an ordinary layer cake, and I promise you will love it. The contrasting crunchy and creamy textures are one of those things that seems like it would be wrong, but is absolutely right. The finished cake is dramatic and quite gorgeous. Make it for a birthday or special event.

1   Preheat the oven to 275°F (135°C). Line two cookie sheets with parchment paper.

2   Using a stand mixer fitted with the whisk attachment, or a handheld electric mixer, beat the egg whites on low speed for 2 minutes, until bubbles start to form.

3   Increase the speed medium-high and whip until the egg whites start to thicken, roughly 2 to 3 minutes.

4   Add the sugar, 1 tablespoon at a time, until it is all incorporated. The egg whites will double in volume and become shiny.

5   Add the cornstarch, vinegar, and cocoa powder and mix for 2 minutes more.

6   Spread a flat 10-inch round disc of meringue on each prepared cookie sheet.

7   Bake for 1 to 1¼ hours. Turn off the oven but leave the meringue in the oven to dry out for 3 hours.

RECIPE CONTINUES

To help you make perfectly round meringue layers, trace a 10-inch pan on the parchment paper and then turn over the parchment so the ink will not be touching the meringue.

8   Meanwhile, whip the cream until stiff peaks form.

9   *To assemble the cake:* Set one meringue disc on a serving platter and generously spread the chocolate mousse on top, followed by half the whipped cream. Place the other meringue disc on top and finish with the remaining whipped cream. Garnish with chocolate shavings. Keep refrigerated and enjoy within 2 days.

A DELICIOUS ETON MESS

MAKES 6 SERVINGS

1 recipe Mum's Fancy Pavlova (page 222), prepared through Step 7

1½ cups (340 milliliters) heavy cream

1½ cups (225 grams) raspberries

½ cup pistachios (71 grams), toasted and finely chopped

NOTE

To bring out all the lovely flavors of the pistachios, it's very important to toast them before using them in this recipe. Spread them over a rimmed baking sheet and toast them in the oven at 350°F (180°C) for about 10 minutes, until lightly golden.

One of the things my mum would make with pavlova was Eton Mess, a mix of broken bits of meringue, whipped cream, fruit, and nuts. While strawberries are traditional for this dessert, my favorite flavor combination is raspberries and pistachios.

1   In a large bowl, break up the meringue round into big and small chunks.

2   Whip the cream until stiff peaks form. Spoon the cream over the meringue chunks and gently mix together.

3   In a separate bowl, roughly mash the raspberries with a fork.

4   Fold half the raspberries and half the pistachios into the whipped cream mixture.

5   To serve, spoon the mixture into six tall glasses, layering it with more mashed raspberries and pistachios. Eat immediately or store in the refrigerator, covered, for up 24 hours before serving.

THREE-INGREDIENT CHOCOLATE MOUSSE

MAKES 6 SERVINGS

2 cups (12 ounces/ 340 grams) chopped bittersweet chocolate

½ cup (115 milliliters) whole milk

6 large (240 grams) egg whites, at room temperature

Whipped cream, for serving

NOTES

For this recipe, I recommend using the freshest eggs available or pasteurized eggs.

As far back as I can remember, my mum has had this old brown cookbook, surely straight out of the 1970s. When I was growing up and learning to bake, I used to thumb through the pages looking for something to make. One of the recipes was for chocolate mousse, and the photograph showed it in a wine glass, layered with whipped cream—I thought it was the fanciest thing I had ever seen. It inspired the version here. It's so easy, but I still think it's one of the most elegant desserts you can make.

1   Put the chocolate and milk in a large heatproof bowl and gently melt in the microwave or over a bain-marie (see page 30). Set aside to cool slightly.

2   Using a stand mixer fitted with the whisk attachment, or a handheld electric mixer, whip the egg whites until stiff peaks form.

3   Fold a spoonful of the egg whites into the chocolate mixture to loosen it. Gently fold in the remaining egg whites until fully incorporated, taking care not to overmix.

4   Divide the mousse evenly among six individual serving dishes. (If not serving immediately, keep refrigerated, covered, for up to 3 days.) When ready to serve, top with a dollop of freshly whipped cream and some chocolate shavings (see page 21).

WHITE CHOCOLATE & MASCARPONE MOUSSE

MAKES 6 SERVINGS

1⅓ cups (8 ounces/ 225 grams) chopped white chocolate

¼ cup (2 ounces/ 57 grams) mascarpone cheese

¼ cup (57 grams) sugar

½ cup (115 milliliters) heavy cream

1 vanilla bean, halved lengthwise

3 large egg whites, at room temperature

1 cup (5 ounces/ 142 grams) raspberries, for serving

NOTES

For this recipe, I recommend using the freshest eggs available or pasteurized eggs.

Use the best-quality ingredients you can find for this recipe, and you'll be rewarded with a sweet and creamy mousse with the heady aroma of vanilla that comes from using a whole vanilla bean. I like to serve this portioned into individual bowls, each topped with fresh raspberries, but a topping of roasted strawberries (see page 112) also pairs nicely.

1   Melt the white chocolate in a small heatproof bowl in the microwave or over a bain-marie (see page 30). Set aside to cool slightly.

2   In a large bowl, combine the mascarpone, sugar, and cream. Scrape the vanilla seeds into the mixture and whisk until smooth and slightly thickened.

3   Using a stand mixer fitted with the whisk attachment, or a handheld electric mixer, whip the egg whites until stiff peaks form.

4   Swiftly mix the melted white chocolate into the mascarpone mixture.

5   Gently fold the egg whites into the mascarpone–white chocolate mixture until just combined.

6   Pour the mousse into six small bowls or ramekins and refrigerate for at least 5 hours.

7   Serve with fresh raspberries on top, or store in the refrigerator, covered, for up to 2 days before serving.

LEMON CURD MOUSSE

MAKES 5 SERVINGS

3 large egg whites, at room temperature

½ cup (115 milliliters) heavy cream

2 tablespoons sugar

1 cup (225 grams) Easy Lemon Curd (page 292)

Whipped cream, for serving

1 cup (142 grams) blueberries, for serving

NOTE

For this recipe, I recommend using the freshest eggs available or pasteurized eggs.

Buttery, tart lemon curd is the base for this velvety and quite beautiful dessert. If you have the lemon curd already made in the fridge, you'll be able to whip this up especially quickly. Serve it in individual glasses, topped with whipped cream and fresh bright blueberries.

1   Using a stand mixer fitted with the whisk attachment, or a handheld electric mixer, whip the egg whites on high speed until stiff peaks form. Set aside.

2   In a separate bowl, whip the cream and sugar until soft peaks form.

3   Gently fold the lemon curd into the whipped cream until smooth and fully incorporated.

4   Gently fold in the beaten egg whites.

5   Spoon the mousse into five small serving bowls and refrigerate for at least 5 hours.

6   Serve with whipped cream and blueberries, or store in the fridge, covered, for up to 3 days before serving.

THREE-INGREDIENT NO-CHURN VANILLA ICE CREAM

MAKES 3 PINTS

2 cups (450 milliliters) heavy cream

1 (14-ounce/ 397-gram) can sweetened condensed milk, cold (refrigerate for at least 3 hours or preferably overnight)

2 teaspoons pure vanilla extract

1 vanilla bean, halved lengthwise (optional)

When I was young, I often made a recipe for ice cream that called for only two ingredients—cream and sweetened condensed milk—sometimes adding an ingredient like vanilla extract to intensify its flavor. I still make this ice cream today, and also use the recipe as a blank canvas for a bunch of other desserts, like Brownie Fudge Swirl Ice Cream (page 240) and Boozy Cherry & Pistachio Ice Cream Terrine (page 245). Try tinkering with it yourself to come up with your own flavor combinations.

1 Using a stand mixer fitted with the whisk attachment, or a handheld electric mixer, beat the cream on medium-high speed until soft peaks form.

2 Reduce the mixer speed a little and pour in the cold condensed milk and the vanilla extract.

3 Increase the speed to high again and whip until your mixture is thick and holds stiff peaks.

4 Scrape the vanilla seeds, if using, into the ice cream base and mix until evenly dispersed throughout.

5 Transfer the ice cream base to a large resealable container, cover, and freeze for at least 5 hours or overnight before eating. Store the ice cream in the freezer for up to 6 weeks.

RASPBERRY SWIRL
CHEESECAKE ICE CREAM

MAKES 2 PINTS

½ cup (71 grams) raspberries

1 tablespoon sugar

½ cup (4 ounces/ 115 grams) cream cheese, softened

1 cup (225 milliliters) heavy cream

½ cup (5 ounces/ 142 grams) sweetened condensed milk, cold (refrigerate for at least 3 or preferably overnight)

1 cup (43 grams/ 8 cookies) crushed graham crackers

For this ice cream, the same simple base ingredients as in my Three-Ingredient No-Churn Vanilla Ice Cream (page 236) are transformed into something truly indulgent with the addition of cream cheese, broken bits of graham cracker, and a thick saucy ribbon of raspberry. It's the perfect ice cream for cheesecake lovers.

1   In a food processor, combine the raspberries and sugar and process until pureed. Strain the mixture through a fine-mesh sieve set over a bowl to remove the seeds. Set aside.

2   Using a stand mixer fitted with the whisk attachment, or a handheld electric mixer, whip the cream cheese on medium-high speed until smooth.

3   Pour in the cream and whip until soft peaks form.

4   Reduce the speed a little and pour the cold condensed milk into the whipped cream. Return the mixer speed to high and whip until your mixture is thick and holds stiff peaks.

5   By hand, fold in the crushed cookies and ripple in the raspberry puree so there are distinct swirls of raspberry throughout the ice cream.

6   Transfer the ice cream to a large resealable container, cover, and freeze for at least 5 hours or overnight before eating. Store the ice cream in the freezer for up to 6 weeks.

BROWNIE FUDGE SWIRL ICE CREAM

MAKES 2 PINTS

⅔ cup (4 ounces/ 115 grams) chopped bittersweet chocolate

1 cup (225 milliliters) heavy cream

½ cup (5 ounces/ 142 grams) sweetened condensed milk, cold (refrigerate for at least 3 or preferably overnight)

1½ cups (115 grams) crumbled brownies

¼ cup (57 grams) Hot Fudge Sauce (page 287)

Mix chunks of brownie into a super-easy ice cream base and then push it over the top by swirling in hot fudge sauce. Really, do I need to say anything else?

1   Melt the chocolate in a small heatproof bowl in the microwave or over a bain-marie (see page 30). Set aside to cool slightly.

2   Using a stand mixer fitted with the whisk attachment, or a handheld electric mixer, whip the cream on medium-high speed until soft peaks form.

3   Reduce the speed a little and pour the cold condensed milk into the whipped cream. Return the mixer speed to high and whip until your mixture is thick and holds stiff peaks.

4   Quickly fold in the melted chocolate (do this swiftly so the chocolate doesn't harden on the cream). Stir in the brownie crumbles and swirl in the hot fudge sauce so there are distinct ripples throughout the ice cream.

5   Transfer the ice cream to a large resealable container, cover, and freeze for at least 5 hours or overnight before eating. Store the ice cream in the freezer for up to 6 weeks.

PEANUT BUTTER & FUDGE ICE CREAM PIE

MAKES 8 SERVINGS

FOR THE OREO COOKIE CRUST

⅔ cup (142 grams) butter, melted

2 cups (170 grams/ 26 cookies) Oreo cookie crumbs (see Note)

FOR THE FILLING

1 cup (225 milliliters) heavy cream

¾ cup (213 grams) sweetened condensed milk, cold (refrigerate for at least 3 hours or preferably overnight)

1 teaspoon pure vanilla extract

⅓ cup (43 grams) salted roasted peanuts, chopped, plus more for serving

⅓ cup (71 grams) smooth peanut butter

1 recipe Hot Fudge Sauce (page 287)

Wickedly sweet and really indulgent, this pie starts with a crushed Oreo cookie crust. I fill it with my Three-Ingredient No-Churn Ice Cream mixed with peanut butter, then serve it with a generous portion of fudge. As my mum always said, "May as well be hung for a sheep as a lamb"—meaning, you might as well go all out, right?

1   *To make the crust:* Grease a 9-inch round cake pan and line it with two layers of plastic wrap (this will make it easy to remove the pie from the pan once it's frozen).

2   In a medium bowl, stir together the melted butter and the cookie crumbs until the mixture has the texture of wet sand. Transfer the crumb mixture to the prepared pan and use your fingertips to press it over the bottom and up the sides of the pan. Refrigerate for 30 minutes to set.

3   *To make the filling:* Using a stand mixer fitted with the whisk attachment, or a handheld electric mixer, whip the cream on medium-high speed until soft peaks form.

4   Pour in the condensed milk and vanilla and whip until your mixture is thick and forms stiff peaks.

5   By hand, stir in the peanuts and then the peanut butter.

6   Pour the filling into the prepared crust and smooth out the surface with a spatula. Freeze for at least 5 hours before serving. (The pie will keep in the freezer, covered, for up to 6 weeks.)

7   Cut into big slices, pour on some hot fudge sauce, and sprinkle with peanuts.

NOTE

Remove the creme center from the Oreos before you crush them—you only need the cookies themselves. Alternatively, you could substitute another brand of chocolate wafer cookies, such as Nabisco Famous Chocolate Wafers.

BOOZY CHERRY & PISTACHIO ICE CREAM TERRINE

2 cups (10 ounces/ 284 grams) pitted cherries, coarsely chopped

1 tablespoon sugar

3 tablespoons Kirsch or other fruit brandy

1 cup (225 milliliters) heavy cream

½ cup (142 grams) sweetened condensed milk, cold (refrigerate for at least 3 hours or preferably overnight)

¾ cup (106 grams) pistachios, toasted and chopped, plus more for garnish

In this recipe, Kirsch, a brandy made with cherry juice, is used to macerate fresh cherries, which are then mixed into my Three-Ingredient No-Churn Ice Cream, along with toasted pistachios. I love to serve this in slices with more of the macerated cherries spooned over the top, which makes it elegant enough for a dinner party. You could easily make this ahead of time and store it in the freezer for a no-fuss dessert ready to serve at any time.

1. In a medium bowl, combine the cherries, sugar, and Kirsch. Refrigerate for at least 2 hours or preferably overnight.

2. Grease a 9 x 5-inch loaf pan and line it with two layers of plastic wrap.

3. Using a stand mixer fitted with the whisk attachment, or a handheld electric mixer, whip the cream on high speed until soft peaks form.

4. Reduce the mixer speed to medium and pour the cold condensed milk into the whipped cream. Whip until it reaches soft peaks.

5. Fold in the pistachios and about half the macerated cherries (1 cup/142 grams). Refrigerate the remaining cherries until ready to serve.

6. Pour the ice cream into the prepared pan, cover, and freeze for at least 5 hours or preferably overnight.

7. To serve, turn the terrine out onto a platter. Spoon over the remaining 1 cup (142 grams) macerated cherries and sprinkle with pistachios. Cut into thick slices. If there are leftovers, store, covered, in the freezer for up to 6 weeks.

NO OVEN NEEDED

WHO NEEDS AN OVEN? WHEN I WAS A KID, I USED TO make a refrigerator biscuit cake (also known as an icebox cake) that only needed to be assembled and then refrigerated for a few hours before serving. I quickly realized that I could create lots of amazing desserts pretty easily without using the oven, which was very useful on really hot days or if the oven was already being used for something else. Recipes like My Family's Favorite Tiramisu (page 257) or The Simplest Rocky Road Fudge (page 249) are great choices if you can't stand the heat but you want to stay in the kitchen. This is also the chapter where you'll find several of my signature mug cakes, "micro-baked" in a microwave, giving you a chance to eat cake without leaving yourself with a bunch of pans in the sink to clean up.

THE SIMPLEST ROCKY ROAD FUDGE

MAKES 12 TO 14
SERVINGS

**3 cups (18 ounces/
510 grams) chopped
semisweet chocolate**

**1⅓ cups (397 grams)
sweetened condensed
milk**

**2 tablespoons
(28 grams) butter**

**2 cups (115 grams)
mini marshmallows**

**¾ cup (106 grams)
salted roasted peanuts,
coarsely chopped**

You know those extra-special desserts? The ones that call your name from the fridge? This is one of those. I learned early on not to leave a knife beside it in the fridge. It was just asking for trouble—I was too tempted to keep slicing off a few nibbles at a time. This is one of the few recipes in my repertoire that calls for semisweet chocolate, which is closer to milk chocolate. It's the best type of chocolate to pair with marshmallow and salty peanuts, resulting in a very rich, seductive candy you won't soon forget.

1   Grease an 8-inch square cake pan and line it with parchment paper.

2   In a large bowl, combine the chocolate, condensed milk, and butter and melt them together in the microwave or over a bain-marie (see page 30). Try not to stir too much, as stirring can cause the fudge to separate.

3   Gently fold in the chopped peanuts and marshmallows, reserving a little of each to be scattered over the top.

4   Pour the fudge into the prepared pan, smooth out the top with a spatula, and sprinkle with the reserved nuts and marshmallows, pressing them gently into the fudge.

5   Cover and refrigerate the fudge for 3 to 4 hours, until it is solid enough to cut into squares.

6   Cut into small pieces and enjoy! The fudge will keep happily in an airtight container at room temperature for up to 2 weeks.

SIMPLIFIED CHOCOLATE TRUFFLES

MAKES 50 TRUFFLES

1¾ cups (10.5 ounces/
298 grams) chopped
bittersweet chocolate

⅔ cup (142 milliliters)
heavy cream

½ cup (1 stick/
115 grams) butter

¼ cup (57 milliliters)
orange liqueur (optional)

⅛ teaspoon salt

Unsweetened cocoa
powder, for dusting

One of the duties of a pastry chef is to make what we call petit fours—really any small after-dinner treat—and I often made truffles. They are easier to make than they look, and guests were always impressed to see a little plate of them on the table after a meal. The recipe here is for a basic chocolate version. I add a little orange liqueur because I think it goes so well with cocoa, but feel free to leave it out.

1   Put the chocolate, cream, and butter in a heatproof bowl and melt them together in the microwave or over a bain-marie (see page 30).

2   Whisk in the orange liqueur, if using, and salt.

3   Pour the truffle mixture into a small dish, roughly 5 x 8 inches. Cover and refrigerate overnight to firm up.

4   Scoop ½-tablespoon portions of the chocolate mixture and roll them into balls. If you find that the chocolate is too hard to scoop, let it sit at room temperature for 30 minutes to soften. Finish the truffles by tossing and rolling them in the cocoa (this is a messy job, but once tossed in cocoa powder the truffles will look great). If you find the truffles are too soft at this point, refrigerate them for about an hour to firm them back up.

5   Store in an airtight container in the fridge for up to 10 days.

GINGERSNAP & CREAM REFRIGERATOR CAKE

2 cups (450 milliliters) heavy cream

1 cup (225 milliliters) fresh orange juice

About 40 store-bought gingersnaps (340 grams), plus gingersnap crumbs for decorating if desired

Here's a cake that couldn't be simpler, but the results are spectacular. I saw this recipe in the back of a magazine when I was a kid. It came out so well, my mum asked me to make it again for one of her dinner parties. It's a typical icebox cake, where all you need to do is dip cookies—in this case, gingersnaps—in orange juice and then layer them in a trifle dish with lots and lots of whipped cream. The cake is then refrigerated until the cookies get soft and the flavors meld together in a really wonderful way. You can make this recipe in one 7½ x 4½-inch trifle dish, but I also like to make it in individual servings for a pretty presentation.

1   Whip the cream until stiff peaks form. Set aside.

2   Pour the orange juice into a shallow dish. One at a time, dip the gingersnaps in the juice, turning them to get both sides. Don't dip them for too long, or the cookies will become too soft. As you work, arrange the cookies over the bottoms of six individual serving dishes. Spoon a layer of the whipped cream over the cookies. Repeat until you've used all the cookies. Finish with a layer of whipped cream on top and garnish with additional cookie crumbs, if you'd like.

3   Refrigerate for at least 2 hours to set before serving. Store in the fridge, covered, for 1 day.

REFRIGERATOR CHOCOLATE BISCUIT CAKE

MAKES 8 SERVINGS

1 cup (6 ounces/
170 grams) chopped
bittersweet chocolate

½ cup (1 stick/
115 grams) butter

¼ cup (57 grams) sugar

2 tablespoons
unsweetened cocoa
powder

3 cups (142 grams)
crushed plain cookies
(such as graham crackers
or digestive biscuits)

½ cup (71 grams) raisins

¼ cup (35 grams)
chopped maraschino
cherries (optional)

Back in Ireland, I used to watch a children's television show called *Blue Peter* when I was a kid, and they would often demonstrate how to cook something. I first saw this recipe on the show and I made it myself all the time after that. It's a mixture of melted butter, cocoa, broken cookies, and dried fruit that is pressed into a loaf pan and refrigerated until it sets. This is a very popular dessert in Ireland; in fact, a big trend there is to have a biscuit cake as one layer of a wedding cake. Or sometimes even the whole wedding cake. It's a great recipe for teaching kids how to cook—it's fast and there's no worry about turning on the oven or stove.

1 Line a 9 x 5-inch loaf pan with plastic wrap.

2 Put the chocolate and butter in a large bowl and melt them together in the microwave or over a bain-marie (see page 30), stirring until melted.

3 Whisk the sugar and cocoa powder into the chocolate mixture. Add the crushed cookies, raisins, and cherries and mix well.

4 Transfer the mixture to the prepared pan and press down firmly with a spatula, making it level on top. Cover and refrigerate for at least 4 hours, or until set.

5 Cut into slices to serve. Keep stored in the fridge, covered, for up to 2 weeks.

MY FAMILY'S FAVORITE TIRAMISU

MAKES 10 SERVINGS

3 large eggs, separated

½ cup (115 grams) sugar

2 cups (16 ounces/ 450 grams) mascarpone cheese

35 to 40 store-bought ladyfingers

2 cups (450 milliliters) strong brewed coffee, cooled

½ cup (115 milliliters) brandy

¼ cup (28 grams) unsweetened cocoa powder

NOTES

For this recipe, I recommend using the freshest eggs available or pasteurized eggs.

One of my mum's staple desserts was tiramisu, and because I love coffee, I also loved that she made it frequently. It's the type of dessert that kids thought was very grown-up and sophisticated. I still love this classic dessert and make it often myself.

1   In the bowl of a stand mixer fitted with the whisk attachment or in a large bowl using a handheld electric mixer, whisk the egg yolks and sugar until the mixture is pale and holds a ribbon on the surface when the whisk is lifted out. Whisk in the mascarpone until the mixture thickens.

2   In a clean mixer bowl using a clean whisk attachment, whisk the egg whites until they form stiff peaks.

3   Gently fold the egg whites into the mascarpone mixture. Refrigerate until ready to assemble.

4   Pour the coffee and brandy into a shallow dish. Dip the ladyfingers into the coffee mixture one at a time and arrange them over the base of a 9 x 13-inch or similar size serving dish. When dipping, do not let the ladyfingers soak, or they will get soggy; instead, dip one in the liquid and then quickly turn and dip the other end, then straight into the serving dish.

5   Spread one-third of the mascarpone mixture over the ladyfingers, covering them well, then repeat the layers twice more, dipping the ladyfingers, arranging them in the dish, and then covering with mascarpone.

6   Refrigerate for at least 5 hours to set. Before serving, dust generously with the cocoa powder. This is best eaten within 24 hours.

SINGLE-SERVING KEY LIME PIE CHEESECAKE

MAKES 6 SERVINGS

FOR THE COOKIE CRUST

2 cups (170 grams/ about 25 to 30 cookies) gingersnap cookie crumbs

¾ cup (1½ sticks/ 170 grams) butter, melted

FOR THE FILLING

1 cup (8 ounces/ 225 grams) cream cheese, softened

¾ cup (7½ ounces/ 213 grams) sweetened condensed milk

Grated zest and juice of 5 Key limes, plus additional zest for garnish, if desired

1 cup (230 milliliters) heavy cream

These little Key lime cheesecakes are a great make-ahead dessert. Made in single-serving glasses, they have all the flavorful and textural elements of a full-size pie, and look impressive, too.

1 *To make the cookie crust:* In a small bowl, stir together the cookie crumbs and the melted butter. Divide the crumb mixture among six individual serving dishes and press down gently. Refrigerate for about 30 minutes to set.

2 *Meanwhile, to make the filling:* Using a stand mixer fitted with the whisk attachment, or a handheld electric mixer, beat the cream cheese, condensed milk, lime zest, and lime juice on high speed until smooth.

3 Add ½ cup (115 milliliters) of the cream and beat until the mixture stiffens.

4 Divide the cream cheese mixture among your serving dishes. Cover and refrigerate for at least 5 hours to set. (The cheesecakes can be stored in the fridge for up to 3 days before serving.)

5 Just before serving, whip the remaining ½ cup (151 milliliters) cream. Transfer the whipped cream to a piping bag fitted with a large star tip and pipe a rosette on top of each cheesecake (or spoon a dollop of whipped cream on top of each). Garnish with a little lime zest, if you'd like.

LEMON MERINGUE TRIFLE

1 recipe Mum's Fancy Pavlova (page 222), prepared through Step 7

2½ cups (565 milliliters) heavy cream

1 cup (85 grams/ 8 cookies) graham cracker crumbs

6 tablespoons (¾ stick/ 85 grams) butter, melted

1 recipe Easy Lemon Curd (page 292)

Deconstruct a lemon meringue pie, and you'll have this fantastic trifle, with all the flavors and none of the fussiness of the original. The layers of lemon curd, crushed cookies, broken-up pieces of meringue, and lots of whipped cream make it a simply gorgeous dessert that is as bright and sunny as a summer day.

1   Roughly crumble up the meringue into big and small pieces.

2   Whip the cream until stiff peaks form. Set aside.

3   In a medium bowl, mix together the graham cracker crumbs and melted butter.

4   To assemble: Dollop some whipped cream over the bottom of a large serving dish, then follow with a layer of crumbled meringue, some more whipped cream, a layer of lemon curd, and then the graham cracker crumbs. Repeat to make three layers, then finish with more whipped cream and graham cracker crumbs. Be generous with the meringue, as there is lots of it.

5   Refrigerate for at least 4 hours before serving. Store leftovers in the fridge, covered, for up to 2 days.

SUNDAY'S LEMON CHEESECAKE

MAKES 12 SERVINGS

3 cups (270 grams/ 24 cookies) graham cracker crumbs

1 cup (2 sticks/ 225 grams) butter, melted

2 teaspoons powdered gelatin

4 teaspoons water

3 cups (24 ounces/ 675 grams) cream cheese

⅓ cup (75 grams) sugar

Grated zest and juice of 3 lemons, plus a couple of lemon slices for decorating, if desired

1½ cups (355 milliliters) heavy cream

Whipped cream, for decorating (optional)

NOTE

If you don't have a piping bag, you can use a zip-top plastic bag to pipe the whipped cream instead. Transfer the whipped cream to the bag and cut the tip off one corner for piping.

On Sundays when I was young, Mum would make a roast dinner for lunch. Dessert was often lemon cheesecake. She would hand me, my brother, or one of my sisters a bag of digestive biscuits and a rolling pin and we would get down on our hands and knees on the kitchen floor and bash them to bits, which my mum would then use to make the crust. The filling was a mixture of cream cheese, whipped cream, and a block of lemon jelly, a packaged, premade Jell-O-like product that doesn't seem to be easily found in the US. At that time, I thought it the height of sophistication. I've tried to make my recipe taste just like Mum's.

1   In a medium bowl, mix together the cookie crumbs and butter. Press the mixture firmly over the bottom of a 9-inch springform pan. Cover and refrigerate for 30 minutes to set.

2   Put the gelatin in a small bowl. While whisking, pour in the water and mix until smooth. Set aside for 5 minutes to allow the gelatin to soften (or "bloom"). It will look spongy when it's ready.

3   Using a stand mixer fitted with the whisk attachment, or a handheld electric mixer, beat the cream cheese, sugar, lemon zest, and lemon juice until smooth.

4   Pour in the cream and whip for 3 to 4 minutes, until the mixture has thickened.

5   Heat the gelatin in the microwave for 15 to 20 seconds, until it is in liquid form. Set aside to cool slightly. Swiftly incorporate the cooled gelatin into the cream cheese mixture (you'll want to do this quickly so the gelatin doesn't set before it's incorporated).

6   Pour the filling over the prepared crust and smooth with a spatula. Cover with plastic wrap and refrigerate overnight to set.

7   If you'd like, decorate the cheesecake by piping rosettes of whipped cream on top and placing a few thin slices of lemon in the center. Store the cheesecake in the fridge, covered, for up to 3 days.

"IN CASE OF EMERGENCY" 1-MINUTE MICROWAVE BROWNIE

MAKES 1 MUG BROWNIE

3 tablespoons all-purpose flour

3 tablespoons light brown sugar

3 tablespoons unsweetened cocoa powder

⅛ teaspoon salt

3 tablespoons vegetable oil

3 tablespoons water

½ teaspoon pure vanilla extract

2 teaspoons chocolate chips

Vanilla ice cream, for serving

A fan once requested a recipe for a cake made without an oven, something I initially thought impossible. But then it dawned on me: *Why not use a microwave?* It took a lot of experimentation, but once I perfected the recipe, it turned out to be the most requested recipe I've ever created. It's fudgy and chocolaty, and the only hard part is stopping yourself from eating it while it's still too hot. Many people have been skeptical, but all I can say is, you will be pleasantly surprised. It's really good, and you don't need to worry about eating too much because it makes only one serving!

1   In a medium microwavable mug, mix together the flour, brown sugar, cocoa powder, and salt.

2   Pour in the oil, water, and vanilla and mix until just combined. Stir in the chocolate chips. (If you don't want to cook the brownie straight away, you can refrigerate it for up to 24 hours at this point; the cooking time will be the same.)

3   Microwave for 45 to 60 seconds, until risen and firm to the touch. This timing is based on my 1,200-watt microwave, so your timing may vary. Always keep a close eye on your mug while it's in the microwave so the brownie doesn't overcook.

4   Serve warm, with vanilla ice cream.

CONFETTI MUG CAKE

MAKES 2 MUG CAKES

2 tablespoons (28 grams) butter

1 large egg

2 tablespoons whole milk

1 teaspoon pure vanilla extract

¼ cup (57 grams) sugar

6 tablespoons (57 grams) self-rising flour (see page 304)

1 tablespoon sprinkles, plus more for decorating

Birthday Cake Buttercream Frosting (page 276), for serving

Did you have a great day at work, or do you simply want to share something sweet with someone special? These festive little cakes are just right for a party of two. This is where self-rising flour comes in handy, keeping these mini treats light. You won't believe these cakes could come out of a microwave until you make them yourself.

1   Place the butter in a large microwavable mug and microwave for 20 to 30 seconds, until melted.

2   Add the egg and whisk well. Add the milk, vanilla, and sugar and stir to combine.

3   Add the flour and sprinkles and stir with a fork until smooth.

4   Divide the batter between two mugs. (If you don't want to cook the cakes straight away, you can refrigerate them for up to 24 hours at this point.)

5   Microwave each mug separately for 50 seconds, or until the cake is risen and firm on top. This timing is based on my 1,200-watt microwave, so your timing may vary. Always keep a close eye on your mug while it's in the microwave so the cake doesn't overcook. Let cool completely before frosting.

6   Once cooled, pipe or spread a swirl of Birthday Cake Buttercream Frosting onto each cake, decorate with sprinkles, and enjoy!

JELLY DOUGHNUT IN A MUG

MAKES 1 MUG CAKE

2 tablespoons (28 grams) butter

1 large egg yolk

1 tablespoon whole milk

¼ cup all-purpose flour

2 tablespoons sugar

½ teaspoon baking powder

¼ teaspoon ground cinnamon

2 tablespoons strawberry jam

Cinnamon-sugar, for garnish

Once I perfected making cakes in mugs, it didn't take long for me to wonder if I could make a doughnut using the same technique. The experiment was a big success, and this recipe turned out to be a favorite of my fans; it's light and fluffy, and the jam makes it taste just like a jelly doughnut from a bakery. And since it's not fried, it's an indulgence you don't need to feel too guilty about.

1   Place the butter in a large microwavable mug and microwave until just melted, about 20 seconds.

2   Add the egg yolk and milk and whisk with a fork to combine. Add the flour, sugar, baking powder, and cinnamon and mix until just combined and smooth. Place 1 tablespoon of the jam down into the batter to make a jammy center. (If you don't want to cook the doughnut straight away, you can refrigerate it for up to 24 hours at this point.)

3   Microwave for 45 seconds, or until risen and firm on top. This cooking time is based on my 1,200-watt microwave, so your timing might vary. Always keep a close eye on your mug while it's in the microwave so the doughnut doesn't overcook.

4   Sprinkle some cinnamon-sugar over the doughnut, top with the remaining 1 tablespoon jam, and enjoy!

OOEY-GOOEY
GINGERBREAD PUDDING

MAKES 6 SERVINGS

½ cup (1 stick/
115 grams) plus ⅓ cup
(71 grams) butter

⅓ cup (115 grams)
molasses

1 cup (230 grams) light
brown sugar

1 large egg, at room
temperature

1½ cups (213 grams)
all-purpose flour

1 teaspoon ground ginger

2 teaspoons ground
cinnamon

⅔ cup (142 milliliters)
whole milk

1 teaspoon baking soda

1 cup (225 milliliters)
water

Vanilla ice cream,
for serving

This incredibly moist and aromatic dessert is almost like magic. As the cake steams in a slow cooker (yes, a slow cooker!), it rises up, creating two layers—cake on top and pudding on the bottom. You *must* serve it warm with vanilla ice cream—you'll thank me later.

1   Put ½ cup (115 grams) of the butter, the molasses, and ½ cup (115 grams) of the brown sugar in a medium heatproof bowl and gently heat in the microwave or over a bain-marie (see page 30) until just melted. Set aside to cool slightly.

2   Swiftly whisk in the egg.

3   Sift the flour, ginger, and cinnamon over the molasses mixture and gently whisk to combine.

4   Heat the milk in the microwave or in a small saucepan until warm to the touch. Stir the baking soda into the warm milk to activate it; you will see bubbles form.

5   Whisk the milk into the molasses mixture until just combined.

6   Pour the batter into a 4-quart slow cooker.

7   In a small saucepan or in the microwave, heat the remaining ⅓ cup (71 grams) butter, the water, and the remaining ½ cup (115 grams) brown sugar until the butter has melted and the sugar has dissolved. Gently pour the butter mixture over the gingerbread batter. It will be hot, but that's okay.

8 Place the lid on the slow cooker and cook on High for about 2 hours, until the cake is firm in the middle and no wet batter is visible. (This baking time is based on my slow cooker; your timing may vary depending on the strength of yours.)

9 Remove the slow cooker insert and set aside to cool slightly.

10 Serve the pudding warm, with vanilla ice cream—you will be in heaven! Store leftover pudding in the fridge, covered, for up to 4 days.

SALTED CARAMEL & PEANUT CHOCOLATE TART

MAKES 12 SERVINGS

FOR THE GRAHAM CRACKER CRUST

⅔ cup (10 tablespoons/ 142 grams) butter, melted

2 cups (170 grams/ 16 cookies) graham cracker crumbs

FOR THE FILLING

½ cup (115 grams) salted roasted peanuts, coarsely chopped

1 cup (283 grams) My Signature Salted Caramel Sauce (page 288)

½ recipe Rich Chocolate Ganache (page 284), warm enough to be pourable

Making this tart couldn't be easier. The crust is pressed into the pan with your fingers—no rolling out dough or prebaking needed. The saltiness of the peanuts balances the intensity of the chocolate ganache, resulting in an amazing tart that's perfect with a dark cup of coffee after dinner.

1 *To make the crust:* Grease a 9-inch tart pan and line it with two layers of plastic wrap (this will make it easy to remove the tart once it's set).

2 In a medium bowl, stir together the melted butter and the graham crumbs until the mixture resembles wet sand.

3 Press the crumb mixture over the bottom and up the sides of the prepared tart pan. Refrigerate for about 30 minutes to set.

4 *Meanwhile, to make the filling:* In a small bowl, stir together the peanuts and the caramel sauce.

5 Spread the caramel mixture over the crust. Pour the ganache over the caramel layer. Refrigerate for at least 5 hours to set before serving. Keep refrigerated, covered, for up to 4 days.

Chapter 7

BOLD BAKING BASICS

OVER THE YEARS, I'VE FOUND MYSELF MAKING AND using many basic components over and over again. Some are simply essential, like Best-Ever Buttercream Frosting (page 276) and Cream Cheese Glaze (page 280). Some will help if you run out of something and can't get to the store, like DIY Buttermilk (page 308) or DIY Brown Sugar (page 307). Some taste better than what you can find at the store, like Never-Fail Pie Crust (page 296) and Foolproof Puff Pastry (page 299). And some will actually save you money, like DIY Vanilla Extract (page 300). All of these are used one way or another in the book and once you master them, you'll be a better and more confident Bold Baker.

BEST-EVER BUTTERCREAM FROSTING

**MAKES 5 CUPS
(950 GRAMS)**

**1½ cups (3 sticks/
340 grams) butter,
softened**

**6 cups (690 grams)
confectioners' sugar,
sifted**

**3 tablespoons whole
milk**

VANILLA BUTTERCREAM
FROSTING

**2 teaspoons pure vanilla
extract**

**1 vanilla bean, halved
lengthwise and seeds
scraped out (optional)**

CHOCOLATE FUDGE
BUTTERCREAM
FROSTING

**1⅓ cups (152 grams)
unsweetened cocoa
powder**

COFFEE BUTTERCREAM
FROSTING

**1½ tablespoons instant
espresso, dissolved in
2 tablespoons water**

BIRTHDAY CAKE
BUTTERCREAM
FROSTING

**2 teaspoons almond
extract**

**1 teaspoon pure vanilla
extract**

**1 teaspoon liquid green
food coloring**

Once you learn how to make a basic buttercream, you'll find it very easy to make whatever flavor you like. Go classic by adding vanilla as for the All-the-Sprinkles Birthday Cake (page 201), or add coffee like I do for the Strong Coffee & Walnut Toasted Cake (page 198). It's endlessly adaptable. I've included a few variations for you to try, but I encourage you to create your own big and bold flavors.

1   Using a stand mixer fitted with the whisk attachment, or a handheld electric mixer, whip the butter on medium-high speed until light, creamy, and pale in color, about 7 to 8 minutes.

2   Add the confectioners' sugar, one spoonful at a time, and mix each until fully incorporated before adding the next. Add the milk and beat on high speed for 3 to 4 minutes, until the buttercream is very light, creamy, and fluffy.

3   To make flavored buttercream, simply stir in your preferred flavorings at the very end of mixing.

4   Use the buttercream straight away or store it in an airtight container in the refrigerator for up to 4 weeks. Let it come to room temperature before using.

CLOCKWISE FROM TOP: Chocolate Fudge, Vanilla, Coffee, and Birthday Cake Buttercream Frostings

CREAM CHEESE FROSTING

MAKES 5 CUPS
(950 GRAMS)

**1 cup (8 ounces/
225 grams) cream
cheese, softened**

**4 tablespoons
(½ stick/57 grams)
butter, softened**

**3½ cups (402 grams)
confectioners' sugar,
sifted**

**2 teaspoons pure
vanilla extract**

Good all-around cream cheese frosting is a recipe all good
bakers should have in their back pocket. It is a must for
Red Velvet Cake (page 186) and Classic Coconut Cake
(page 189).

1   Using a stand mixer fitted with the whisk attachment,
    or a handheld electric mixer, beat the cream cheese and
    butter on medium-high speed for 3 to 4 minutes, until light
    and fluffy.

2   Slowly add in the confectioners' sugar and beat until the
    frosting is smooth and creamy, then mix in the vanilla.

3   Cover and refrigerate for at least 3 hours before using so
    the frosting is firm enough to spread. Store in the fridge,
    covered, for up to 6 days.

CREAM CHEESE GLAZE

**MAKES ½ CUP
(142 MILLILITERS)**

**¼ cup (2 ounces/
57 grams) cream cheese**

**1 cup (115 grams)
confectioners' sugar**

1 tablespoon whole milk

**1 teaspoon pure vanilla
extract**

This glaze is perfect for My Best-Ever Carrot Cake (page 166) and Cinnamon Roll Cake (page 169). Try it on any baked good that needs a little something extra.

1   Put the cream cheese in a medium bowl and soften it slightly in the microwave for about 20 seconds or over a bain-marie (see page 30). You want it to be soft enough to mix with a spoon.

2   Add the confectioners' sugar, milk, and vanilla and whisk until a smooth glaze is formed.

3   Use immediately, or store in an airtight container in the fridge for up to 5 days.

VANILLA **GLAZE**

MAKES ¼ CUP
(71 MILLILITERS)

⅓ cup (37 grams) confectioners' sugar

1 teaspoon pure vanilla extract

½ teaspoon whole milk (optional)

NOTE

Feel free to get creative and add food coloring or different flavorings to the glaze.

I pour this glaze over Buttery Almond Breakfast Pastry (page 149) while the pastry is still warm to create a crisp, sweet crust. And be sure to drizzle it over the Lemon-Blueberry Loaf (page 170) to elevate the flavor and texture.

1   In a small bowl, whisk together the confectioners' sugar and vanilla until smooth. If you would like the glaze a little thinner, add the milk.

2   Use immediately, or store in an airtight container at room temperature for up to 5 days.

RICH CHOCOLATE GANACHE

MAKES 2½ CUPS
(565 GRAMS)

1½ cups (340 milliliters) cream (see Note)

2 cups (12 ounces/ 340 grams) chopped bittersweet chocolate

NOTES

For this recipe, you can use any type of cream you have on hand.

To reheat the ganache, transfer it to a heatproof bowl and set it over a bain-marie (see page 30) or pop it into the microwave for a few seconds to melt gently.

Ganache is almost endlessly versatile, depending on its temperature. Warm it up, and you can pour it over desserts or dip churros into it. A little cooler, and you can whip it into the perfect frosting. Cooler still, and you can make the easiest of chocolate truffles. The choice is yours.

1   In a small saucepan, bring the cream to a simmer over medium-low heat. Keep an eye on it as it heats—it shouldn't come to a boil.

2   Pour the hot cream over the chocolate in a medium bowl and let sit for 5 minutes to soften and melt the chocolate.

3   Stir the ganache until smooth, then let cool and use warm, at room temperature, or cold as specified in your recipe. Store in an airtight container in the fridge for up to 2 weeks.

HOT FUDGE SAUCE

**MAKES 2 CUPS
(450 MILLILITERS)**

½ cup (57 grams)
unsweetened cocoa
powder

½ cup (115 grams) sugar

½ cup (115 milliliters)
heavy cream

4 tablespoons (½ stick/
57 grams) butter, cut
into pieces

⅛ teaspoon salt

½ teaspoon pure vanilla
extract

With a jar of hot fudge sauce in the refrigerator, you'll always
be ready to embellish a dessert, whether it's a simple bowl of
vanilla ice cream or my Peanut Butter & Fudge Ice Cream
Pie (page 242).

1 In a small saucepan, combine the cocoa powder, sugar,
   cream, and butter.

2 Cook over medium heat, whisking continuously, until the
   butter has melted and the mixture comes to a simmer.
   Reduce the heat to low heat and simmer, whisking often,
   for about 3 minutes more. Remove from the heat and stir
   in the salt and vanilla.

3 Let cool slightly before using, or let cool completely
   and store in an airtight container in the fridge for up to
   6 weeks.

MY SIGNATURE
SALTED CARAMEL SAUCE

**MAKES 1½ CUPS
(340 GRAMS)**

1 cup (225 grams) sugar

**½ cup (115 milliliters)
water**

**½ cup (115 milliliters)
heavy cream**

**6 tablespoons (¾ stick/
85 grams) butter, cubed**

¼ teaspoon salt

NOTE

Making caramel
takes practice, but
don't be put off.
Follow my steps
and I guarantee you
success. You got
this!!!

Just as we add condiments to savory foods to enhance their flavors, you can think of this caramel sauce as a condiment for desserts. It has the perfect balance of sweetness and saltiness that will keep you wanting just one more spoonful. I experimented quite a bit to reach that perfect combination, and I think you will love it as much as I do. I always have a jar in the back of my fridge for dessert emergencies.

1 Heat the sugar and water in a medium saucepan over medium-low heat, without stirring and without letting it simmer, until the sugar has dissolved.

2 Increase the heat to medium and bring the mixture to a simmer—do not stir the mixture once it comes to a simmer, or it may crystallize. Cook, without stirring, until the mixture becomes an amber-colored caramel, roughly 6 to 7 minutes. Be careful not to let the caramel smoke or burn.

3 Immediately whisk in the cream. Since the cream is colder than the caramel, the mixture will bubble and/or splatter, but keep on whisking and it will dissolve.

4 Whisk in the butter. Simmer the caramel for 1 minute. Remove from the heat and stir in the salt.

5 Let cool slightly before using, or let cool completely, then store in an airtight container in the refrigerator for up to 12 weeks.

SIMPLE PASTRY CREAM

**MAKES 3 CUPS
(675 GRAMS)**

**2 cups (450 milliliters)
whole milk**

**½ vanilla bean, halved
lengthwise**

½ cup (114 grams) sugar

**4 large egg yolks,
at room temperature**

**¼ cup (58 grams)
cornstarch**

**2 tablespoons
(28 grams) butter,
cut into small pieces**

A wonderful creamy filling for profiteroles and other pastries, this classic French pastry cream is one you'll use all the time. It's particularly good for tarts and pies.

1 Pour the milk into a medium saucepan. Scrape the vanilla seeds into the milk, add the pod, and add ¼ cup (57 grams) of the sugar. Bring to a simmer over medium-low heat.

2 Meanwhile, in a medium bowl, whisk together the egg yolks, cornstarch, and remaining ¼ cup (57 grams) sugar.

3 While whisking constantly, slowly pour one-third of the hot milk mixture into the egg yolk mixture to temper the yolks. Pour the tempered egg mixture back into the saucepan and cook over medium-high heat, whisking continuously, for 2 to 3 minutes, until the mixture thickens.

4 Remove from the heat and whisk in the butter.

5 Strain the mixture through a fine-mesh sieve into a clean bowl to remove the vanilla pod and any bits of cooked egg. Cover the pastry cream with plastic wrap, pressing it directly against the surface to prevent a skin from forming. Refrigerate for at least 4 hours or up to 4 days before using.

EASY LEMON CURD

**MAKES 2 CUPS
(284 GRAMS)**

½ cup (115 grams) sugar

Grated zest and juice of
4 large lemons

2 tablespoons cornstarch

1 large egg plus 3 large
egg yolks, at room
temperature, beaten

6 tablespoons (¾ stick/
85 grams) butter, cubed

Lemon curd is well-known for giving lemon meringue pie its zesty, sweet punch, but its intense flavor can also turn practically any dessert on its head—in a very good way. If you have this on hand in the fridge, you'll always be able to whip up a dessert that will definitely get noticed.

1   In a medium saucepan over medium heat, combine the sugar, lemon zest, and juice and bring to a simmer.

2   In a small bowl or measuring cup, mix ¼ cup of the hot lemon mixture with the cornstarch. Then swiftly whisk the cornstarch mixture back into the saucepan and cook, whisking as the mixture simmers, for 2 to 3 minutes. Reduce the heat to low.

3   While whisking, working quickly, add the eggs and butter (do this quickly so the eggs don't cook before they're incorporated). Cook for 3 minutes more, or until thick. Remove from the heat.

4   Strain the lemon curd through a fine-mesh sieve into a clean bowl to remove the zest and any bits of cooked egg. Press a sheet of plastic wrap directly against the surface to prevent a skin from forming and set aside to cool.

5   Use immediately or store in the fridge for up to 2 weeks.

FRANGIPANE

**MAKES 2 CUPS
(450 GRAMS)**

¾ cup (1½ sticks/
170 grams) butter

¾ cup (170 grams) sugar

1½ cups (170 grams)
almond flour or almond
meal

3 tablespoons
all-purpose flour

2 large eggs, beaten

1 teaspoon almond
extract

Several recipes in this book call for frangipane, a sweet pastry cream made with ground almonds (one of my favorite flavors). It is a beautiful complement to fruit, like in My English Bakewell Tart (page 137) and Blueberry & Almond Galette (page 133); I also use it on its own in my Buttery Almond Breakfast Pastry (page 149).

1   Melt the butter in a medium heatproof bowl in the microwave or over a bain-marie (see page 30).

2   Stir in the sugar, almond flour, flour, eggs, and almond extract.

3   For the best results, chill the frangipane for at least 2 hours to firm up before using.

4   Store in an airtight container in the fridge for up to 2 weeks.

NEVER-FAIL PIE CRUST

**MAKES ENOUGH
DOUGH FOR ONE
9-INCH SINGLE CRUST**

1⅓ cups (185 grams)
all-purpose flour

1 tablespoon
confectioners' sugar

⅛ teaspoon salt

7 tablespoons
(99 grams) cold
butter, cubed

1 large egg yolk

3 tablespoons cold water

A crucial recipe to have in your repertoire is a pie crust you can count on. I have traveled far and wide and worked at many jobs, and this crust recipe, which I've used since I was a kid, has been with me through thick and thin. It makes a buttery, flaky crust, and it's the only recipe I use for pies, tarts, and galettes. I guarantee you will use this recipe so often, it will become the most tattered and butter-stained page in this book.

1   In a large bowl, stir together the flour, confectioners' sugar, and salt.

2   Add the butter and rub it into the dry ingredients with your fingers or a pastry blender until the mixture resembles coarse bread crumbs.

3   In a small bowl, mix together the egg yolk and water. Add to the flour mixture.

4   Bring the dough together with your fingers to form a ball. If the dough is too dry, add a little more water, but do so sparingly—you don't want the dough to be too wet. Wrap the dough in plastic wrap and refrigerate for at least 30 minutes to allow the gluten to relax before rolling. (If not using immediately, the dough can be stored in the refrigerator for up to 3 days or frozen for up to 8 weeks.)

5   On a lightly floured work surface, roll out the dough to your desired size, shape, and thickness (a good thickness is ¼ inch). Fit the dough into your pie or tart pan and bake as directed in the recipe.

FOOLPROOF **PUFF PASTRY**

MAKES 1 LARGE SHEET
PUFF PASTRY

**10 tablespoons
(115 milliliters) water,
chilled**

**1 tablespoon fresh
lemon juice**

**2⅓ cups (325 grams)
all-purpose flour**

⅛ teaspoon salt

**14 tablespoons
(1¾ sticks/200 grams)
butter, frozen for at
least 2 hours**

NOTE

Frozen butter is my
secret ingredient.
The colder the
butter, the flakier
the pastry.

This is my mum's recipe. It's not as labor-intensive as
traditional puff pastry, which calls for endless folding and
rolling. The key is to grate in frozen butter instead. Some
call this a "rough" puff pastry, but the end result is pretty
close to the classic. It can be used in both sweet and savory
recipes, so it's quite versatile.

1   In a measuring cup, mix together the water and lemon
    juice; set aside.

2   In a large bowl, mix together the flour and salt.

3   On the large holes of a box grater, grate the frozen butter
    directly into the flour. Mix the butter through the flour
    until combined.

4   Add the liquid, using your hand to bring the dough
    together until it forms a ball (you may not need all the
    liquid—hold some back just in case you don't need it all).
    If the dough is too wet, it will not be flaky.

5   Wrap the dough in plastic wrap and refrigerate for at least
    1 hour or up to 3 days, or freeze for up to 4 weeks.

DIY VANILLA, COCONUT & ALMOND EXTRACTS

When using extracts in your baking, I want you to think of them like other seasonings, like salt or pepper. Not only do they add their own wonderful flavors, they also bring out the flavors of the other ingredients they are mixed with, making whatever you are baking taste better. I started making my own vanilla extract because I use so much in my recipes and it's very easy to make at home. Plus, it tastes much better than store-bought. Once you try it, I'm sure you'll agree. **MAKES ½ CUP (115 MILLILITERS)**

VANILLA EXTRACT

3 vanilla beans

½ cup (115 milliliters) vodka

1 Cut the vanilla beans in half, then split open each half to expose the vanilla seeds on the inside of the pod.

2 Place the vanilla beans in a small bottle or jar. Add the vodka.

3 Seal the bottle tightly and store in a cool, dry place for 5 to 6 weeks, until the extract reaches your desired flavor. Every few days, flip the bottle upside down to gently mix the liquid inside.

4 Store in a cool, dry cupboard; it will keep indefinitely. Leave the vanilla beans in the bottle for stronger flavor. For an endless supply of vanilla extract, keep on topping up with vodka as the extract gets low.

COCONUT EXTRACT

3 tablespoons unsweetened shredded coconut (fresh or dried)

½ cup (115 milliliters) vodka

1 Place the coconut in a small bottle or jar. Add the vodka.

2 Seal the bottle tightly and store in a cool, dry place for 5 to 6 weeks, until the extract reaches your desired flavor. Every few days, flip the bottle upside down to gently mix the liquid inside.

3 Strain the extract through a fine-mesh sieve into a spouted measuring cup and discard the coconut.

4 Return the extract to the bottle or jar, seal, and store in a cool, dry cupboard; it will keep indefinitely.

ALMOND EXTRACT

14 unsalted raw almonds, chopped

½ cup (115 milliliters) vodka

1 Place the almonds in a small bottle or jar. Add the vodka.

2 Seal the bottle tightly and store in a cool, dry place for 5 to 6 weeks, until the extract reaches your desired flavor. Every few days, flip the bottle upside down to gently mix the liquid inside.

3 Strain the extract through a fine-mesh sieve into a spouted measuring cup and discard the almonds.

4 Return the extract to the bottle or jar, seal, and store in a cool, dry cupboard; it will keep indefinitely.

NOTES

You can replace the vodka with bourbon, but note that it will have a stronger flavor.

For an alcohol-free extract, use 3 parts food-grade liquid glycerin to 1 part water instead of the alcohol (in the recipes above, that's 6 tablespoons glycerin plus 2 tablespoons water).

DIY CAKE FLOUR

**1 cup (142 grams)
all-purpose flour**

2 tablespoons cornstarch

Cake flour is a softer kind of flour. As its name indicates, it's really good for making cakes because they will bake up softer and fluffier, which is what you want in a cake. I call for it in my All-the-Sprinkles Birthday Cake (page 201). If you don't have any at home, you can use this recipe to make your own; multiply the recipe to make as much as you need.

1   Remove 2 tablespoons of the flour, then add the 2 tablespoons of cornstarch back in. Sift together well.

2   Transfer the flour to an airtight container. Label it with the type of flour and the date so you remember what it is and when you made it. Use within 12 weeks.

DIY SELF-RISING FLOUR

**MAKES 1 CUP
(142 GRAMS)**

**1 cup (142 grams)
all-purpose flour**

**2 teaspoons baking
powder**

Sometimes a baked good like my Sticky Toffee Pudding (page 206) needs a little something extra to help it rise properly. Self-rising flour is all-purpose flour with a bit of baking powder mixed in. It's used in recipes that don't call for much leavening—so you wouldn't use it for making bread, but it works really well in My Best-Ever Carrot Cake (page 166).

1 Sift the flour and baking powder together into a bowl to make sure the baking powder is thoroughly and evenly distributed.

2 Transfer the flour to an airtight container. Label it with the type of flour and the date so you remember what it is and when you made it. Use within 12 weeks.

DIY BROWN SUGAR

MAKES 1 CUP

LIGHT BROWN SUGAR

1 cup (225 grams) sugar

1 teaspoon molasses

DARK BROWN SUGAR

1 cup (225 grams) sugar

2 teaspoons molasses

If you are anything like me, you run out of brown sugar when you really need it most. It's easy to make at home and here I've given variations so you can make both light and dark brown sugar.

1 In a medium bowl, combine the sugar and molasses. Using your fingertips, rub the molasses into the sugar until the molasses is completely incorporated and the sugar turns brown.

2 Store in an airtight container at room temperature for up to 1 year. Because of the moisture in the molasses, brown sugar has a tendency to clump together. To prevent this, add a marshmallow to the container; it will keep the sugar dry and fine.

DIY BUTTERMILK

**MAKES 1 CUP
(225 MILLILITERS)**

**2 tablespoons fresh
lemon juice or distilled
white vinegar**

**1 cup (225 milliliters)
whole milk (see Note)**

NOTE

For this recipe, you
need to use fresh
dairy milk. Soy,
coconut, or nut
milks will not work.

Buttermilk is a key ingredient for recipes like Devil's
Food Cupcakes (page 174) and Christopher's Buttermilk
Pancakes (page 87). It's used all the time in Ireland in baking,
resulting in ultra-moist baked goods with a pleasant tangy
flavor—particularly in breads. I'm always being asked how
to substitute for it, since most people don't keep it on hand
in their fridge. When you realize how easy it is to make at
home, you'll probably stop buying it like I did.

1   In a small measuring cup, stir the lemon juice or vinegar
    into the milk. Let sit at room temperature for at least
    30 minutes, until the milk begins to curdle and becomes
    acidic.

2   Use in place of buttermilk in recipes as directed. If not
    using it straight away, store it in an airtight container in
    the fridge for up to 3 days.

DIY SWEETENED CONDENSED MILK

**MAKES 1½ CUPS
(425 MILLILITERS)**

4 cups (900 milliliters) milk (see Notes)

1⅓ cups (296 grams) sugar

NOTES

You can use whole, low-fat, or even nondairy milk to make condensed milk.

A sugar substitute like stevia will not work in this recipe, as it does not caramelize.

When you forget to buy it, you can make sweetened condensed milk at home. I use it all the time, particularly in Three-Ingredient No-Churn Vanilla Ice Cream (page 236) and Single-Serving Key Lime Pie Cheesecake (page 258). It keeps in the fridge for months.

1   In a heavy-bottomed medium saucepan, combine the milk and sugar and cook over medium heat, stirring, until the sugar has dissolved. Reduce the heat to low and bring the mixture to a simmer. Do not stir the mixture once it starts to simmer, or it may crystallize.

2   Gently simmer for 45 to 50 minutes, until the milk has become a rich, creamy color, and has reduced by half and thickened slightly. You may notice some foam forming on the surface as it simmers; gently skim it off with a spoon. (If there is undissolved sugar hanging around the rim of your pot, don't stir it into your condensed milk; this can also cause crystallization.) Take care not to reduce the milk too much, or the fat will separate.

3   Remove from the heat and pour the milk into a jar to cool completely. Seal the jar and refrigerate for a few hours before using (the milk will thicken up a lot as it chills).

4   Label the jar with the date and store in the fridge for up to 6 months.

BAKING CONVERSIONS

WEIGHT

7 grams = ¼ ounce

9 grams = ⅓ ounce

14 grams = ½ ounce

19 grams = ⅔ ounce

21 grams = ¾ ounce

28 grams = 1 ounce

57 grams = 2 ounces

85 grams = 3 ounces

115 grams = 4 ounces

142 grams = 5 ounces

170 grams = 6 ounces

198 grams = 7 ounces

225 grams = 8 ounces

255 grams = 9 ounces

283 grams = 10 ounces

311 grams = 11 ounces

340 grams = 12 ounces

368 grams = 13 ounces

396 grams = 14 ounces

425 grams = 15 ounces

454 grams = 16 ounces

LENGTHS

⅛ inch = 3 millimeters

¼ inch = 6 millimeters

½ inch = 1¼ centimeters

1 inch = 2½ centimeters

2 inch = 5 centimeters

2½ inches = 6 centimeters

4 inches = 10 centimeters

5 inches = 13 centimeters

6 inches = 15¼ centimeters

12 inches = 30 centimeters

OVEN TEMPERATURES

500°F = 260°C

475°F = 245°C

450°F = 230°C

425°F = 220°C

400°F = 200°C

375°F = 190°C

350°F = 180°C

325°F = 165°C

300°F = 150°C

275°F = 135°C

250°F = 120°C

225°F = 110°C

BAKING WITH A CONVECTION OVEN

The general rule when using a convection oven, in which the air is circulated with a fan, is to set the oven temperature 25°F (15°C) lower than what the recipe calls for using in a regular oven. Even then, don't go strictly by cooking time, as ovens vary; rather, be sure to check on the food regularly to see how fast it is cooking.

ACKNOWLEDGMENTS

THANKS TO MY FRIENDS AND FAMILY from far and wide for the support you gave me during the creation of this book. A lot of you didn't see me for months on end but your messages and calls were greatly appreciated. From Ireland to Canada, Australia, and the U.S., thank you for the moral support.

I had a rock-star team for the book photography that was a joy to work with. Thank you Kate Martindale for the master class in styling. You are a force and my favorite Rose buddy. Thank you to the talented Carla Choy for capturing my foods' beauty in your photography and for being the sane person on set. Ali Summers, thank you for being a cool and calming presence during the shoot. Thank you Olivia Crouppen for the tremendous hard work you put into this book and for all the help you gave me over the process. I know it wasn't easy.

To my agent, Maria Ribas, thank you for the hand-holding. I needed it, being a first-time author. You made the process much easier for me to handle. P.S. You are one tough cookie.

To my editor, Stephanie Fletcher, I feel very fortunate for the opportunity to work together with you and the whole HMH publishing team. Thank you for making my dream a reality I'm so proud of.

To my coauthor, Amy Treadwell, every recipe has a story, and thanks to you I was able to tell mine.

I deliberately saved the best for last.

Kevin, without your vision, passion, and incredible hard work there would be no Bigger Bolder Baking. And although I constantly remind you during stressful times that this was all your idea . . . I'm glad it was. Thank you for pushing me, and for your unconditional support and love. I couldn't have done this without you . . . seriously!! Like not even a little bit . . .

Thank you all,

INDEX

Note: Page references in *italics* indicate photographs.